The Marriage Maker

WHAT TIME IS IT IN YOUR MARRIAGE?

Pastor Gregory R. Ojeda

Copyright © 2019 Gregory R. Ojeda

All rights reserved. No part(s) of this book may be reproduced, distributed or transmitted in any form, or by any means, or stored in a database or retrieval systems without prior expressed written permission of the author of this book.

ISBN: 978-1-5356-0743-8

Acknowledgements

I am amazed about what is called "Amazing Grace." This second book about the topic of marriage is all about my Lord, and not about me. I cannot take any credit, nor will I boast about what I have accomplished. I give God the glory for His Amazing Grace.

During the eight months that it took me to pen the content of this book it has been a great privilege to be a vessel in the potter's hands. The words just seemed to flow from heaven to earth as God deposited from His heart to mine His precious treasure. All I can say is, "I stand amazed about Grace."

Can a tool build a structure by itself? No! Can a vessel pour forth of its own accord? No! Can a channel produce fresh water for others to enjoy? No! Neither can I except by His Amazing Grace.

I would like to acknowledge my precious wife, Marilyn Dawn Sabo Ojeda. She has made our journey an "oasis" in the desert. She is my partner, my friend, my confidante, and my better half. My words are not adequate to express my love and appreciation for her as my bride, my greatest fan, and my intimate lover. I love you, honey bun.

I want to thank my manly four boys: Jason, Abe, Josh, and Ben. I could not be more proud to be your father. All of my boys have made fatherhood and family a wonderful experience. I also want to say thank you to the best grandchildren in the world: Karlina, Chelsea, Connie, Alina, JC, and AJ. You make Grandpa proud!

I would like to thank Bishop Ed Ram, my pastor, for his support, encouragement, friendship, and brotherly love. Also I want to acknowledge and thank Pastor Martin Cantu, who I can truly say is a great friend and supporter of my writings. Thanks, Martin!

I would like to thank all my family and friends at Family Celebration Center; you make pastoring a joy. Your help, support, prayers, and love during my illness have been beyond compare. I thank God for His Healing Presence. Look what the Lord has done!

Last of all, I would like to thank the three special couples who helped me pilot this book by being the first participants in this study.

Their names are as follows:
    Martin and Lani Cantu
    Horacio and Ana Angel
    Hector and Patricia Fulgencio

These precious couples have been gracious and teachable. They were honest and transparent, which made it a pleasure to help guide them through this blessed union called marriage.

Contents

How To Use This Book 9

CHAPTER ONE: Once Upon A Time 11

CHAPTER TWO: Batteries Not Included 23

CHAPTER THREE: What Time Is It? 37

CHAPTER FOUR: The Watchpital Marriage 53

CHAPTER FIVE: Don't Throw It Away! 69

CHAPTER SIX: Takes A Licking And Keeps On Ticking 81

CHAPTER SEVEN: Time To Choose Wisely 91

CHAPTER EIGHT: All We Have Is Time 103

CHAPTER NINE: A Time Of Happiness 113

About The Author 127

Foreword

When Pastor Greg shared his first book, titled *What In The World Was God Thinking? "Marriage,"* with me I honestly thought it was just another book on marriage. Over the years I have read plenty on the subject and really didn't want to read another one. Because of my deep respect for both Greg and Marilyn, and the fact that I have known them both for years and know that after many years of marriage they are still crazy in love with each other, I decided to see what Pastor Greg had to say. Wow! When I began reading, I was in awe at the wisdom of this man who had found the keys to making relationships work! I was so overwhelmed that I immediately bought several copies, pledging to never officiate another wedding unless the couple agreed to read his book.

As if that weren't enough, Pastor Greg writes a second book, *The Marriage Maker*. The truths in this book take marriage to a whole new level. It will strengthen any marriage regardless of where two people are at in their relationship. *The Marriage Maker* is the playbook for the Super Bowl game of marriage. To attempt to play the game without the playbook is simply insane.

Pastor Scott Mulvey
Lead pastor, City Church
Northern California District Superintendent,
Grace International

INTRODUCTION

TO ME MARRIAGE IS THE most wonderful, the most exhilarating, and the most challenging relationship all wrapped into one. God has fashioned and framed it for durability for those who venture within the walls of its glory and splendor. If I had it to do all over again, I'd say, "Sign me up!"

I always say that "Marriage is not for the faint of heart," because it takes Courage, Commitment, and Character to guard this precious treasure from God. This "Warrior and Princess" union calls for toughness and tenderness, strength and submission, honor and humility, to conquer the world given to its responsibility.

Marriage itself is supposed to reflect God's unfailing love and commitment for His people, the church. God blending two individuals into one is a wonder and awe for those who behold its mystery. For this reason I have asked the Lord to reveal how to teach and explain this sacred union.

Marriage is what you make it; it can be good or bad, blessing or burden, heaven or hell. The choice is yours. God has given to us the truth, formula, and steps to make our journey together on earth a joyful experience to last a lifetime.

Many marriages in America are full of miserable couples. Why? They are not applying the principles of God's word, which produces peace, harmony, and stability. They would rather gripe about their marriage situation and the daily drama it seemingly produces. To you I say, "This book is for you." To those who dread going home after a hard day at the office, I say, "This book is for you," and to those who would like to vacation alone on a tropical beach,

I say, "This book is for you!" Call me crazy, but I don't believe God instituted the marriage relationship to make us miserable, but rather to bless us. Even though this book resembles a fairy tale, it is not. You can have a "happily ever after" in your marriage relationship. All you have to do is trust the One who designed this fragile timepiece. Marriage itself is complicated yet simplistic, mysterious yet comprehensible. Marriage is a miracle because the hands of the miracle worker has left His fingerprints upon it. It is indeed a "blessed union."

This book has been designed to minister to married couples and those who are single who want to prepare themselves for marriage.

"Always remember: In marriage, You always have a dance partner, You can always drive in the commute lane, You always have a dinner date, and You always have a warm bed." To this I say, amen. ENJOY!

How To Use This Book

Dear friends: I am so blessed to have you take the time to invest in your primary relationship, your marriage. I want to personally thank you for purchasing this book for the purpose of enhancing, enriching, and edifying your marriage. If you are single, I want to thank you for purchasing this book because you desire to prepare yourself for marriage.

The book you are holding has been written to be user-friendly and practical, thought-provoking and inspirational, heavenly and earthly. I am thoroughly convinced that any marriage can be alive, vibrant, and all God intended it to be. All it requires is for any couple to "take the time" to learn and grow together by applying God's truth to their relationship.

Success in marriage is experienced when we understand that God is the "Marriage Maker," and he knows what makes marriage "tick!" The delicate and intricate workings of the marriage relationship are sustained and preserved through the wisdom of His word, the Bible. This relationship is an earthly journey that has its highs and lows, good and not-so-good experiences we share together. However, one thing is for sure: "marriage is what you make it." It is up to us to follow the principles and pattern as outlined in the scriptures to make marriage last a lifetime!

This book has been provided to fit any setting and format—it can be an easy read by yourself or a guide for a couple in need of a tune-up. It can be a workbook for a small group or for a large group of couples. Its content is "one size fits all," and has been designed to help any marriage, whether you are engaged, newlyweds, or have been married for years.

The final page of each chapter will provide simple questions from the chapter you have just studied. This will allow each couple to reiterate and reinforce what they have just learned. Let's take the journey to a land where we can find laughter, fulfillment, and comfort through God, the "Marriage Maker."

Thank you for purchasing this book. My sincere prayer is that through this study your marriage will be enriched, enlightened, and enabled.

Chapter One

ONCE UPON A TIME

ONCE UPON A TIME...

...IN A DISTANT KINGDOM, THERE lived a watchmaker. He labored each day creating, repairing, and restoring watches into elegant works of art. As you passed by his business, regardless of the time, you could peer into the iron-framed front window and find him meticulously working.

He treated each invention as a prized treasure that bore his name and reputation. After all, his fingerprints and handiwork told the story of his care and devotion for every watch that he touched. As he closes each finished timepiece, he sets in motion the hands on the watch towards a brighter future.

The distant kingdom is heaven, the maker is God, and the elegant timepiece is called marriage. Just as the watchmaker cherished time and beauty through his passionate care and love for his profession, so God placed beauty and passion within the cherished union, marriage. The word of God reveals the reason for its being and the eternal message of God's great sacrificial love for his people.

The truth about marriage and what makes it tick is no fairy tale. It begins in the book of Genesis, where Adam declares that a man shall leave his father and his mother, and shall cleave unto his wife, and ends in the book of Revelation at the marriage supper of the Lamb. It begins in Genesis at the tree of knowledge of good and evil, which poisoned the marriage relationship, and ends in the New Testament at the tree called the Old Rugged Cross, where the relationship is restored.

Marriages throughout America and the world have lost their identity, passion, and purpose. The time is now to speak the truth of God's word and his divine intention concerning marriage.

It will take nothing less than the hands of a precision creator to reach into its inner workings to repair and restore it back to its original state. Let's take a closer look into the mind of God, the "Marriage Maker."

(Genesis 1:27–28 KJV) 27 So God created man in his own image, in the image of God created he him; male and female created he them.

28 And God blessed them, and God said unto them, be fruitful, and multiply, and replenish the earth, and subdue it: and have dominion over the fish of the sea, and over the fowl of the air, and over every living thing that moveth upon the earth.

IMAGE: We must always remember that marriage is God's idea. He created, fashioned, and instituted the sacred union to reflect and be an extension of his heavenly kingdom. The influence of our culture and society has muddied and stained the dress of a beautiful bride and stripped the groom of his influence and position. According to the scripture the image of God is found in both the male and female relationship. The image of God is simply the "character" of God imparted. Our identity can only be found in the image of God that we were created in.

WHAT IS IDENTITY? The condition of being oneself or itself, and not another. It is God's original intention. When God creates us he does not make any mistakes. Thousands in our society are confused concerning their gender. The scripture gives us an answer for every question.

(Romans 9:20 NLT) "No, don't say that. Who are you, a mere human being, to argue with God? Should the thing that was created say to the one who created it, "Why have you made me like this?"

Our identity is tied to our gender. What are the first words spoken at the birth of an infant? "It's a boy!" or "It's a girl!" The image of God was marred at the fall of mankind, not changed!

The Bible says that Adam and Eve were created in the image of God, which means that God placed within them the capacity to accomplish all that he had created them to do. Through the power of God's presence and holiness they could imitate and live by the standard of God's moral purity and fulfill the purpose for which they had been placed on the earth.

However, when they disobeyed God's command, sin entered and the purity of the relationship was contaminated. Rather than run to God because of their shame, they ran from him. Their hearts no longer beat in unison with the Marriage Maker and their thoughts betrayed them concerning God's original plan for the first couple.

GOD'S TRUTH CONCERNING MARRIAGE

1. God recognizes only the male and female relationship
2. God blesses only the male and female relationship
3. Only the male and female relationship can be fruitful and multiply
4. Only the male and female relationship can fill the earth
5. God gave influence and dominion over the earth to the man and woman
6. Only the man and woman can become one flesh

WHAT DOES THIS MEAN?

Without the promotion and protection of the marriage union, our society, culture, and world will gradually deteriorate and self-destruct. We must listen to the words of Jesus that solidifies this truth.

(Matthew 19:4–8 KJV)

4 And he answered and said unto them, Have ye not read, that he which made *them* at the beginning made them male and female,

5 And said, For this cause shall a man leave father and mother, and shall cleave to his wife: and they twain shall be one flesh?

6 Wherefore they are no more twain, but one flesh. What therefore God hath joined together, let not man put asunder.

7 They say unto him, Why did Moses then command to give a writing of divorcement, and to put her away?

8 He saith unto them, Moses because of the hardness of your hearts suffered you to put away your wives: but from the beginning it was not so.

In this story Jesus was asked about what circumstance is permissible in order to divorce your companion. Even though he only addressed this one area it can be applicable in other areas also. Jesus' answer was the condition of their hearts. They had simply lost their way concerning God's plan and truth and their hearts were hardened and calloused. What was Jesus' final conclusion?

FROM THE BEGINNING IT WAS NOT SO!

If you want to know something's original purpose, ask its creator! If you don't know the purpose of a thing, misuse is inevitable. He took them back to Eden, God's original purpose. God made them male and female, period! He left no room for clauses, misunderstandings, or misinterpretations.

God's original purpose in marriage was for us to fulfill His divine plan and fill the earth with people after our own kind. Satan did not destroy God's original plan; he only postponed it. Through the coming of the Son of God to the earth, Jesus set in motion the restoration of God's intended purpose for mankind.

The time has come for husband and wife, man and woman, male and female, to take their position and role in God's great calling on earth to which we have been sent.

GOD'S SEQUENCE AND ORDER IN MAN'S CREATION

(Genesis 2:7 KJV) And the LORD God formed man *of* the dust of the ground, and breathed into his nostrils the breath of life; and man became a living soul.

The scripture declares that God chose to create the male first because he would be the protector, defender, and the covering of his counter-part, woman. This truth is understood because when the man was formed, the woman was hidden deep within him, yet unformed. This reveals that Adam was the pace-setter, the trail-blazer, and the initiator in the relationship. Therefore the question we must ask is, "What was Adam's primary purpose in creation?"

1. To walk with God
2. To cultivate and keep the garden
3. To prepare a place for the woman

(Genesis 2:21–22 KJV)

21 And the LORD God caused a deep sleep to fall upon Adam, and he slept: and he took one of his ribs, and closed up the flesh instead thereof;

22 And the rib, which the LORD God had taken from man, made he a woman, and brought her unto the man.

The next question we must ask is, "What is the woman's primary purpose in creation?"

1. To walk with God and Adam
2. To enjoy the garden
3. To rest in the place prepared for her

Woman would be the responder, the supporter, and the beauty in the relationship. Does this imply that the male is superior over the female? Absolutely not! But it does reveal the different roles and functions of the man and the woman.

The scripture then reveals an important aspect concerning the marriage relationship and care for the family.

(Genesis 2:23–25 KJV)

23 And Adam said, This *is* now bone of my bones, and flesh of my flesh: she shall be called Woman, because she was taken out of Man.

24 Therefore shall a man leave his father and his mother, and shall cleave unto his wife: and they shall be one flesh.

25 And they were both naked, the man and his wife, and were not ashamed.

When God presented the woman unto the man his natural response was to declare the nature and purpose of the relationship. Adam did not stutter or look for words to speak. It came naturally because of the order of creation and God's purpose declared back to God by those whom he had created. The first words spoken in the relationship came from the man over the woman.

1. "She shall be called woman" (man with a womb). This declares that the woman is the receiver in the relationship.
2. "Because she was taken out of man." This speaks of the order and nature of the relationship.

3. "Therefore shall a man leave his father and mother, and shall cleave unto his wife, and they shall be one flesh." Notice that it was not the woman that would leave father and mother, but the man. She would simply go from one kingdom (covering) to another. The man would leave to prepare (create) another kingdom.

4. "And they were both naked, and were not ashamed." The man's declarations of position, purpose, and preparation over the woman allowed her to abandon herself to her husband.

THE POWER OF WORDS, IT'S UP TO YOU!

Ok, men, we are the influencer in our family, therefore we must be cautious about the words we speak over our homes. We form a prison or a palace by our words. Proverbs 18:21 says, "The tongue can bring death or life; those who love to talk will reap the consequences." This scripture reveals the power of the words we choose to speak and declare that our words can be life-giving or destructive. I've always believed that we choose our words and then our words choose our future.

OUR WORDS CAN CREATE BLESSINGS OR STOP BLESSINGS!

The words you speak today will form your tomorrow. Jesus Himself solidifies this truth in (Mark 11:22–23 KJV) 22 Have faith in God! 23 For verily I say unto you, That whosoever shall say unto this mountain, Be removed, and be cast into the sea; and shall not doubt in his heart, but shall believe that those things which he said shall come to pass; he shall have whatsoever he said.

Notice that Jesus mentions believing once but mentions speaking three times. Active faith not only involves acting on God's word but first continually speaking God's word. The question we must ask here is, "What is faith?"

1. Faith is believing in the unseen and the unknown

2. Faith is acting out the scripture

Doubt is speaking what we see; faith is speaking what we do not see. It is impossible to exhibit faith without doing something according to the scriptures. Jesus did not say have faith in faith, but have faith in God! We must not only trust that God knows what's best for us, but that he will deliver to us what is best for us. (Luke 12:32b KJV) says, "It is your father's good pleasure to give you the kingdom." The scripture says in (Hebrews 11:1 KJV) "Now faith is the substance of things hoped for the evidence of things not seen." Notice that we are to have faith for the future and we are to believe in what we do not see. Which means that faith is not for today, it is for tomorrow. We are to use our faith today and leave the results to God tomorrow! I challenge all the men who are reading this book to begin speaking blessing and provision over your homes and families. If you are living in lack and your children are not serving the Lord, do not speak what you see, but what you don't see. Believe the blessing of Abraham is for you!

WHAT IS THE BLESSING OF ABRAHAM?

(Genesis 12:2 KJV) And I will make of thee a great nation, and I will bless thee, and make thy name great; and thou shalt be a blessing:

THE LAW OF BLESSING
SPEAK THESE BLESSINGS OVER YOUR FAMILY!
"I WILL"

God has determined to bless me. You can bank on it, expect it to happen, and stake your life on it. The scripture says God cannot lie!

God's favor is upon me, his hand is upon me, and his joy is in me!

It's a set-up. The fight is fixed; I can't possibly lose. It is written!

"MAKE OF THEE"

The word "make" in Hebrew means "To do, to work, to appoint, to prepare, to bring about." God has appointed me to succeed and flourish. God has fashioned and formed me into an honorable vessel.

"A GREAT NATION"

You have to see it before you receive it. You have to speak it before you have it. You have to walk in it before it manifests. God had placed a nation inside of Abraham. He had the ability, and the potential. Why? God had already spoken it!

"AND I WILL BLESS THEE"

God is blessing me right now! It's not a feeling; it's a position. However, when you make it your position, it becomes a feeling, and becomes a confidence.

"AND MAKE THY NAME GREAT"

NAME: reputation, fame, glory

Whenever a believer in the scripture called on the name of the Lord, they called themselves, the God of Elijah, the God of Moses, the God of David.

GOD'S REPUTATION IS AT STAKE!

GREAT: to grow up powerful, become great or important, promote, do great things.

So many believers are trying to promote themselves, make themselves a person of importance, or become a person of power.

(Proverbs 27:2 Parallel Bible) Let another man praise thee, and not thine own mouth; a stranger, and not thine own lips.

Let's allow God's kingdom message and purpose to be fulfilled because we believe and speak according to his will.

SPEAK THIS OUT LOUD: "GOD BLESS MY FAMILY"

CHALLENGE: Sit down as a couple and revisit when you first met. Let each partner share some of the characteristics and special moments that drew you together.

TIME TO SUM IT ALL UP!

1. Write one word that summarizes Chapter One.

2. If you were a counselor, what advice would you give to a struggling couple after you read Chapter One?

3. Did you learn anything new?

4. Circle the correct statements concerning marriage:
    a. God does not recognize only the male and male relationship
    b. God blesses only the male and female relationship
    c. Only the male and female relationship can be fruitful and multiply
    d. Only the male and female relationship can fill the earth
    e. God gave influence and dominion over people
    f. Only the man and woman can become one flesh

5. What was Adam's primary purpose?

6. What was Eve's primary purpose?

7. Finish this quote
Our words can _____ blessings or _____ blessings.

8. What is the blessing of Abraham?

9. What does the name "Woman" mean?

Chapter Two

BATTERIES NOT INCLUDED

Chestnuts roasting on an open fire
Jack Frost nipping at your nose
Yuletide carols being sung by a choir
And folks dressed up like Eskimos

Everybody knows a turkey and some mistletoe
Help to make the season bright
Tiny tots with their eyes all aglow
Will find it hard to sleep tonight

They know that Santa's on his way
He's loaded lots of toys and goodies on his sleigh
And every mother's child is gonna spy
To see if reindeers really know how to fly

And so I'm offering this simple phrase
To kids from one to ninety-two
Although it's been said many times, many ways
Merry Christmas to you

Do you recognize the song and the season? It's my favorite time of the year as we celebrate the birth of Christ. When we were children we could hardly sleep on the night of Christmas Eve. All the kids in our family anticipated the arrival of Old Saint Nick (Santa Claus) and gifts around the tree stacked to the ceiling filled with toys, toys, toys!

I remember my brothers and sisters waking up and rushing to sit at our parents' bedroom door. What were we waiting for? My dad to wake up! All of a sudden the door would open and my dad would appear with his fancy smoking jacket (robe) then we would all run to the living room.

One by one my dad would begin to call our names written on the gifts. By the time he handed us one we would tear off the wrapping and the fun would begin! Darts guns, bouncing balls, toy cars, board games, girly dolls, and records. It was a zoo!

Then I noticed there was one present still under the tree with my name on it. I ran as fast as I could and tore off the paper, and guess what it was? A pink tricycle! Did that matter to me? No, I was the owner of a bike! Before you start laughing, I need you to know I was only five years old.

Now let's fast-forward to my children's generation. The scenario is just the same, only I am the one in the funny robe! My kids are gathered around the artificial Christmas tree and waiting for dear old Dad. As I call out their names they dive in head first. Before you know it, the gift is unwrapped, as they wait for another. Remote-controlled trucks, Simon game, radios, Operation, Tickle Me Elmo, robots, Batmobile, and the list goes on!

There's only one difference between the toys of my generation and my children's generation. We did not need batteries and every toy my kids received did.

I remember the disappointment on their faces as they opened their gifts and read the outside of the box: "Batteries not included!" They simply looked at Mom and Dad and asked, "You bought the batteries, right?" We looked at each other, shrugged our shoulders, and said, "I thought you bought them." What did this mean to our kids? No power, no mobility, no fun!

The toys sat lifeless, still in the box, and to the kids, useless without the batteries. Even if we opened them, they really did not want to play with them, because "BATTERIES NOT INCLUDED."

Our marriages are a lot like these toys that require batteries in order to operate. We must come to the conclusion that marriage does not come with batteries. Many times when a couple enters marriage, they think all they have to do in order to have a thriving marriage is nothing! Their focus rather is on themselves, and the question they often ask is, "What can you do for me?" God created, instituted, and blessed marriage, then gave us the responsibility to care for, protect, and cultivate it. That's right, most couples don't read the fine print when they tie the knot on that special day: batteries not included!

(James 1:17 KJV) Every good gift and every perfect gift is from above, and cometh down from the Father of lights, with whom is no variableness, neither shadow of turning.

In the beginning, God's plan was to create a beautiful garden paradise, but there was only one thing that was holding up the project: there was no one to take care of it. Let's read it for ourselves. (Genesis 2:5 KJV) And every plant of the field before it was in the earth, and every herb of the field before it grew: for the LORD God had not caused it to rain upon the earth, and *there was* not a man to till the ground

God's blessings and gifts from above are truly wonderful, but once he bestows and places them in our hands it then becomes our responsibility to keep, cherish, and manage them.

The batteries in our marriages represent the effort and strength we put into our relationship to make it alive and powerful. (Proverbs 12:27 AMP) The lazy man does not catch *and* roast his prey, But the precious possession of a [wise] man is diligence [because he recognizes opportunities and seizes them.]

Because marriage is a precious possession, I want to focus on one word in this text: it is the word "diligence." This word has several definitions, but the best description I have ever read is "a constant, careful, steady, effort."

CONSTANT: Not changing or varying; uniform; regular; invariable, persistent.

Being constant simply means that we are consistent in our attitude and behavior. It implies a devotion that cannot be swerved. In order to better our marriage relationship we must have a consistency in applying what we learn. We are not moody or constantly changing like the weather. As a pastor, I am always ministering to couples in need of guidance. There have been times when the husband or wife entered a session like a chameleon. I never knew what color they would be, blue, red, yellow, white, or black! It was a revolving door of emotions and suspense.

The reason this area is so important is because without consistency there can be no stability.

CAREFUL: Cautious in one's actions: Be careful when you cross the street.

(Ephesians 5:15–17 KJV) 15 See then that ye walk circumspectly, not as fools, but as wise, 16 Redeeming the time, because the days are evil. 17 Wherefore be ye not unwise, but understanding what the will of the Lord is.

The word "circumspectly" is taken from two words. "Circum," which means around or about. The second word is "specere," which means to inspect or look around. Put them both together, and what do you get? "Watch where you are walking!" This implies paying attention to our marriage relationship by protecting it and treating it as a precious treasure.

We must walk with our eyes wide open, pay attention to our steps, and live life intentionally. This means we are to think before we act or make a decision, considering the repercussions of our choices and whom it will affect.

The book of Hebrews gives us insight pertaining to the choices we make. (Hebrews 11:26 CSB) For he considered reproach for the sake of the Messiah to be greater wealth than the treasures of Egypt, since his attention was on the reward.

The word "considered" is the key in the matters of making important decisions that can alter our life. "Considered" means counting the cost, to weigh or measure, to think from up to down before making a decision. Moses had a choice to make concerning whether to assume his future position as the next pharaoh or reveal his real identity as a Hebrew slave. If he chose the latter, he would forfeit the riches, authority, and the right to lead a world empire. It was at this point that Moses looked at the consequences of his choice. He gazed down the road of life in his mind and saw the destruction and sorrow he would experience if he chose the counterfeit riches of Egypt. He weighed in the balance the brief suffering he would experience if he chose to serve Jehovah and deny the ways of the world. What was the conclusion? The riches of Christ and eternity were of greater value than the pleasures of sin for a moment.

As a married couple we must always be careful to "consider" the choices, actions, and decisions we make. We must always look down the road in our minds and count the cost of our decisions before we make them.

WE MUST ASK OURSELF...

Whom will this decision affect?

Will it bring bondage or freedom?

Will it lead me into truth or error?

Will it lead me into holiness or sin?

Will it create unity in my marriage or division?

Will it bring me closer to Christ?

Once you answer these personal questions, you then can make your choice with confidence that God will be glorified and your family protected. We must always remember that when we make choices, we are not the only ones that are affected. Those around us whom we influence will be convinced to do the same. The married couple that bases all their decisions, choices, and plans on the wisdom of God's word will have great influence to impact the world around them.

When we fail to apply God's word, it is as if we are functioning as a toy without batteries. No power, no mobility, no fun! It's disobedience that kept the children of Israel wandering in the wilderness for forty years. God led them to the brink of the promise and allowed them to see it. They stood there at the Jordan and viewed what God said could be theirs. They tasted a sample of the sweet fruit of the land that a few men brought back from the land of God's promise. There was only one thing that kept them from moving forward: they had no batteries!

No guts, no heart, no courage, and, most of all, no love for God! Just think, you can have the best marriage ever, God's Garden of Eden in your heart and home. You can taste the Lord and experience that he is so good! What's stopping you? No batteries!

God split the Red Sea, but Israel had to walk across. Jesus healed the lame man from birth, but he had to get up by himself, take his bed, and walk!

Actually, the only person that's stopping you is you. Jesus Himself even said, "The gates of hell would not prevail" against us. We cannot blame our spouse, boss, friends, circumstances, or even the devil! The time is now, the place is where you are, and the person is you!

The next word is "steady," which means firm, consistent and unchanging.

(Hebrews 12:28 KJV) Wherefore we receiving a kingdom which cannot be moved, let us have grace, whereby we may serve God acceptably with reverence and godly fear.

We must realize the things in the world are unsteady and cannot be trusted. They are here today and gone tomorrow; therefore the only reliable source on which our lives and relationships must be built are the principles and truths of the Kingdom of God.

In order to be steadfast in your marriage you must build it upon the foundation of the word of God. Much effort and patience must be something we practice on a daily basis. One thing I learned decades ago is that God is not in a hurry as he interacts and relates to us, so why should we be in a hurry as we interact and walk with our mate? My advice to you is to take your time, enjoy the journey, and look for the special moments that can strengthen your relationship.

DO YOU REMEMBER?

It is always a blast when my wife will bring out the family album. Beehive hair-dos, platform shoes, plaid sport coats, and those first pictures after you were born—ugly! What do those pictures represent? A special moment in time, an event to embrace, and a precious memory in the past caught in a picture!

These freeze-frame moments pass us by daily. I believe in our lifetime we miss hundreds of opportunities to bond, affirm, and share our love with our spouse and family. Once you miss it you cannot rewind, start over, or repeat, but have missed a space in time that you cannot regain. What is the answer?

LOOK FOR A KODAK MOMENT!

Remember the Polaroid camera? You took the picture and then you had to wait for it to develop right before your eyes. As it began to materialize we realized why it was called a Kodak moment.

As we look to build bridges from heart to heart we must treat our eyes like a camera lens. Kids have a baseball game or a ballet recital? Look for a Kodak moment. Attending a special event or wedding? Look for a Kodak moment. Kids or spouse have a birthday? Look for a Kodak moment! Get the picture?

My wife and I were once at a birthday party when her favorite love song began to play. She stood up like a princess awaiting her prince to sweep her off her feet. The only problem was, her prince had turned into a frog. After all, there were about twenty other people in the room and some of them were strangers! What was my problem? Pride and nervousness (and boy was I uncomfortable) kept me from a Kodak moment. That event was about fifteen years ago and I regret it to this day. If I had to do it all over again I would have rescued my princess. Marilyn is just the opposite of me. She does not only look for a moment to celebrate, she knows how to create it.

Which brings me to the next question I want to ask you. How many of you celebrate your family's birthdays? I know lots of people that couldn't care less if they acknowledged the day their mate or their children were brought into this world. My wife is one that doesn't want a birthday party on her special day. I always tell her, "If you don't want it, I will take it!"

Is there anyone else out there who doesn't want theirs? I'll take yours also! On April 12, which is my birthday, in case you want to know, I want the biggest party ever. When my wife sends out the invitations I always tell her to end it with "Monetary gifts appreciated!" I'm sorry, but I don't want T-shirts, funny-looking sweaters, or even slippers; cash will do, yeah!

In our family, Marilyn always makes a big deal about all our children's and grandchildren's birthdays. My boys are now forty-five, thirty-seven, thirty, and twenty-eight, and we still give them birthday parties. It is a special time of recognition, attention, sharing love, and food!

Let me encourage all you husbands, wives, and families out there: make it a special day for each individual's birthday, anniversary, graduation, promotion, and see what happens. It will be a time of strengthening relationships, caring, loving, and healing. It's called celebration!

When I was growing up we never ate dinner at the kitchen table. We always ate in the living room on TV trays! Why? So we could watch TV! I know what you're thinking and I've heard it over and over, but my favorite episode of *The Andy Griffith Show*, *Happy Days*, *I Love Lucy*, and *Sanford and Son* is on!

When Marilyn and I were first married she mentioned a few times how nice it would be if we sat at the dinner table. As our family grew from one son to two to three and finally four, nothing had changed. We were definitely a fast-food family: McDonald's, Taco Bell, Foster Freeze, Jack in the Box, and the list goes on. What could be better? Just drive up, eat in your vehicle or at home in front of the television, and everyone's full! The only question is, full of what?

However, every once in a while Marilyn would lure us all into the dining room. Then a strange thing occurred while we were enjoying our meal: we actually began to talk and converse with each other. I often wondered why this setting was conducive to strengthening relationships.

As I continued to study the Bible, I discovered something wonderful about this subject. Jesus did not spend most of His time in the synagogue, but around the dinner table! As a matter of fact, the Bible states that much of the ministry of the Son of God was spent eating his way through the gospels.

He ate with publicans and sinners, had two picnics where he fed four thousand people and then five thousand. He ate often at the home of Mary, Martha, and Lazarus. What we must realize here is mealtime was not just about food.

According to Bible customs, wars were settled, covenants were made, friendships were strengthened, and peace was shared at the table of the Lord. The disciples understood this truth all too well because much of our Lord's teachings revolved around dining with Jesus and others. No wonder that the Lord's last days on earth revolved around food, which meant intimacy, relationships, caring, comfort, faith, and spiritual rest.

The Last Supper was nothing new to his disciples because it simply was solidifying the previous times shared in the past three and one half years. It was then that I realized that the Lord's Table did not just refer to communion, but sharing in the common-union that we shared daily with Christ in our homes.

The meals of fellowship with Jesus were not something that began in the New Testament. It was merely a continuation of the seven Old Testament Feast Celebrations that lasted eight days, while others lasted twenty-one days, which of course included lots of eating. Wow, does God love to party! Each feast told the story of God's eternal plan and the work that Christ came to accomplish.

Jesus was fulfilling the essence of what Israel's attitude should have been, which was joy, celebration, and thanksgiving.

After the death of Jesus there are two scriptural accounts that give additional insight. The first is found in Luke 24:13–32. Two of his disciples travelled on the road to Emmaus while discussing all the previous events that led to the death of Jesus.

While they talked, Jesus himself appeared and began to walk with them. The only thing was, he somehow turned off their recognition center so they would not know it was him. The journey from Jerusalem to Emmaus was about two hours. I can imagine the conversation they had, the doubts, the unanswered questions, and the fears that filled their hearts and minds.

They convinced the stranger to stay overnight as their guest. Then something amazing happened. As Jesus sat at dinner, He blessed the bread and broke it. As soon as he did, their eyes were opened and they beheld Him with their own eyes; then he disappeared! Then they declared, "Did not our hearts burn within us as he talked with us and opened unto us the scriptures?" Bewildered and confused, the disciples went back to their previous occupation, fishing.

ALL THIS HAPPENED AROUND SHARING AND EATING!

Let's read the next account. (Matthew 21:3–6, 9, 12–15 KJV) 3 Simon Peter saith unto them, I go a fishing. They say unto him, we also go with thee. They went forth, and entered into a ship immediately; and that night they caught nothing.

4 But when the morning was now come, Jesus stood on the shore: but the disciples knew not that it was Jesus.

5 Then Jesus saith unto them, Children, have ye any meat? They answered him, No.

6 And he said unto them, Cast the net on the right side of the ship, and ye shall find. They cast therefore, and now they were not able to draw it for the multitude of fishes.

9 As soon then as they were come to land, they saw a fire of coals there, and fish laid thereon, and bread.

12 Jesus saith unto them, Come *and* dine. And none of the disciples durst ask him, Who art thou? Knowing that it was the Lord.

13 Jesus then cometh, and taketh bread, and giveth them, and fish likewise.

14 This is now the third time that Jesus shewed himself to his disciples, after that he was risen from the dead.

15 So when they had dined, Jesus saith to Simon Peter, Simon, *son* of Jonas, lovest thou me more than these?

THEY WENT FROM OBEDIENCE TO BLESSING TO INTIMACY

The words "come and dine" were all too familiar as the disciples rushed to the shore, knowing what to expect: comfort, encouragement, blessing, and food! It is time to fellowship, celebrate, and share at the table of the Lord, "our home!"

These are just a few suggestions that can keep your marriage from being powerless and the hands in your relationship moving in the right direction.

CHALLENGE:

Sit down together with the old family photo album. Talk about where you were, what you experienced, and what you loved about that time in your life.

TIME TO SUM IT ALL UP!

1. Write one word that summarizes Chapter Two.

2. If you were a counselor, what advice would you give to a struggling couple after you have read Chapter Two?

3. Did you learn anything new?

4. What does made in the image of God mean?
    - ( ) a. We are exactly like God
    - ( ) b. We look like God
    - ( ) c. We have been created in the character of God

5. What is identity?
    - ( ) a. It is thinking like God
    - ( ) b. The condition of being oneself or itself, and not another
    - ( ) c. It is being spiritually minded

6. What is one aspect of God's truth concerning marriage?
    - ( ) a. God only recognizes the male and female relationship
    - ( ) b. Marriage is made in heaven
    - ( ) c. God created woman and then created the man

7. Fill in the blanks

God created, instituted, and blessed marriage, then gave us the responsibility to _____, _____ and _____ it.

8. What does the word "diligence" mean?

9. What does "batteries not included" imply?

10. How can you make a Kodak moment?

Chapter Three

WHAT TIME IS IT?

Every April and every October we set our clocks either forward or backward. It's called Daylight Savings Time (or "*fall*ing back" and "*spring*ing forward"). Because we never change the alarm clock in our bedroom, it is correct only six months out of the year. Right now it is the right time; however, when April arrives we are supposed to spring forward one hour, and guess what happens? You guessed it: the time is off by one hour!

The only dilemma is, if your clock is set for fall, when springtime rolls around you will be an hour late wherever you go. One Sunday morning my family and I arrived at church and the parking lot was full. As we entered the sanctuary, it was full of worshippers. My wife and I had a bewildered look on our face when everyone began to laugh, and they asked, "Did you forget to set your clocks forward?" Needless to say, it never happened again—lesson learned!

Time is our most precious commodity. It is valuable and cannot be regained once it has passed by. Regardless of race, gender, social and financial status, everyone has been allotted the same amount of time. God set in motion times, seasons, day and night in the beginning.

(Genesis 1:3–5, 14 KJV)

3 And God said, Let there be light: and there was light.

4 And God saw the light, that *it was* good: and God divided the light from the darkness.

5 And God called the light Day, and the darkness he called Night. And the evening and the morning were the first day.

14 And God said, Let there be lights in the firmament of the heaven to divide the day from the night; and let them be for signs, and for seasons, and for days, and years.

God has gracefully allotted each of us the same amount of time, which is twenty-four hours a day. The effectiveness and quality of our time can be directly related to how wisely we choose to use it. As we interact with one another daily, we must be aware of the principle of time.

The funny thing about time, however, is that we spend most of it trying to convince and change others to think like us. This is never truer than in our marriage relationships. Prior to marriage, during the dating stage, we love everything about our significant other. But once the knot is tied, the habits and behaviors we once thought were cute now become annoying.

One truth in scripture I learned years ago is found in Genesis 1:26. It says that God gave Adam and Eve "dominion" over the birds, fish, and things that crawl on the earth. However, he never gave them dominion over another human being. Wow, that reveals a great principle that should encourage each one of us, which is this: the only person that we are in control of and the only person we can change is ourselves!

The benefit of working and changing yourself is this: when you change yourself, you automatically change your marriage, for the better! Genuine change and transformation comes by accepting the truths of God's word and applying them to our life as the Holy Spirit ignites our hearts. What does this imply? If you see an area that needs to change in your mate, take it to God in prayer and let your petition be poured out with grace and God's love! In turn, the sweet Holy Spirit will gently and lovingly lead your companion into being conformed into the blessed image of their Savior.

HERE ARE 5 WAYS YOU CAN WORK ON YOURSELF AND USE YOUR TIME WISELY

1. IT IS TIME TO BE TOUCHABLE

People that are untouchable are not accessible to others. I see several Prime ministers, CEOs, rock stars, presidents, and even some pastors that consider themselves bigwigs in the world and who choose not to make time for others. I know what you are thinking: there is not enough time, energy, and strength to touch everyone that wants my attention.

To you I present my perspective on this matter. If we want to better ourselves as individuals and become people of impact in this world, we must touch as many people as we can while we are in this world. A great quote to remember is, "You can impress people from a distance, but you can only impact them from close up."

One of the qualities that I admire in our president, Donald Trump, is he knows how to touch the crowd. Just watch him at a charity event, a presidential rally, or a joint congress address. He walks slowly through the crowd pointing his finger, smiling, winking, and laughing to the multitude of people that have come to see him. As I view this I notice one thing: I feel like he is pointing, winking, and smiling at me. The other quality I've observed about his entrance is how often he stops and extends his hand and says, "Hi. What's your name? Thanks for coming, I'm glad you're here." He always addresses individuals by their first name because he wants to be touchable and personable.

The question we must ask ourselves is this: "Was Jesus touchable?" The answer is yes!

(Mark 5:24–31 KJV)

24 And *Jesus* went with him; and much people followed him, and thronged him.

25 And a certain woman, which had an issue of blood twelve years,

26 And had suffered many things of many physicians, and had spent all that she had, and was nothing bettered, but rather grew worse,

27 When she had heard of Jesus, came in the press behind, and touched his garment.

28 For she said, If I may touch but his clothes, I shall be whole.

29 And straightway the fountain of her blood was dried up; and she felt in *her* body that she was healed of that plague.

30 And Jesus, immediately knowing in himself that virtue had gone out of him, turned him about in the press, and said, Who touched my clothes?

31 And his disciples said unto him, Thou seest the multitude thronging thee, and sayest thou, Who touched me?

You see, Jesus allowed the crowd of people to touch him. What I want you to notice is he did not stop for everyone, but he made himself accessible. I truly believe that if the Bible did not record everything that Jesus said and did that there were individuals who were blessed, healed, and set free just by touching him. Jesus did not stop for everyone, but he stopped often!

If you read the Bible it simply says that Jesus would stop in the crowd, extend his hand, and ask, "What's your name? Thanks for coming, I'm glad you're here!"

DON'T MISS THE SMALL OPPORTUNITIES

In one scriptural account there were those in the crowd that had brought their children to Jesus that he might lay his hands on them. Of course the disciples frowned upon this by replying, "Stop. Don't touch him. He doesn't have time. They are not important enough for Jesus to stop!" Naturally, Jesus reprimanded his disciples for this attitude and mindset. Never think that you are too big or too important for the small things in life, you might miss a big blessing!

TAKE A KNEE

I believe as the children approached him he knelt down to get on "their level." I learned how important it was when Marilyn and I ministered in children's church to over eighty children every Sunday for two years to "take a knee" when talking to children. It makes you approachable and easy to converse with.

Here's the lesson, as I take a little liberty and paraphrase the text. I don't think Jesus kneeled on both knees, but he placed "one knee on the ground and one in the air." Remember, Jesus was both God and man. Placing one knee in the air symbolized the matters that pertain to the high and lofty things of God, and placing one knee on the earth that he was human, touchable, and accessible.

There are too many Christians and church leaders who are afraid of losing their "anointing" by allowing others in the crowd to touch them. If you want to be effective as a married couple on the earth, you both need to practice this Biblical advice.

DON'T TOUCH ME!

These are the last words a husband wants to hear from his wife. Prior to marriage you hugged, kissed, embraced, held hands, and reached for her at any given moment. What happened? You blew it! Remember, prior to marriage, you talked all night, you listened intently, and you had continual eye contact. Everything a girl loves, you no longer practice.

Remember this…

    If you want to touch, you have to talk

    If you want to kiss, you have to cuddle

    If you want to love, you have to laugh

2. IT IS TIME TO SAY YES

The Power of Yes

EFFECTIVE WAYS TO UTILIZE TIME AND GET MORE OUT OF RELATIONSHIPS AND LIFE

It is very easy to say "yes" to the things we like to do. You know what I'm talking about: a banana split, buying a new car, or a trip to Hawaii, who could resist? However, how many times, because you don't feel like it, do you say "No" to something when you could have said "Yes"? The word yes sends a positive message and can create opportunities for us to experience a new perspective in our relationships and in life.

My wife Marilyn to this day always tells the boys when they are getting ready to leave the house, say "No" to drinking, "No" to drugs, and definitely say "No" to sex. It is obvious that there are some things we must say NO to. However, my point is, if we want to enhance our relationships and make each day count we must seize the opportunities presented to us by saying "YES."

WHY WAS JESUS SO SUCCESSFUL IN RELATIONSHIPS AND IN MINISTRY?

HE KNEW HOW TO SAY YES!

I'M THANKFUL THAT JESUS SAID YES BEFORE HE FULLY UNDERSTOOD ALL THAT HE WOULD EXPERIENCE.

GREAT WAY TO PRAY: "Good morning Lord, Yes! I say Yes to your purpose, Yes to your inconveniences, to your challenges, and Yes to your perfect will!

(MATTHEW 8:1–34)

1. LEPER (vs 1–3)

2. CENTURION'S SERVANT (vs 5–10)

3. PETER'S MOTHER-IN-LAW WAS SICK (vs 14–15)

4. AT EVENING THEY BROUGHT THE DEVIL POSSESSED AND THOSE THAT WERE SICK (vs 16)

5. HE REBUKED THE WIND AND THE SEA AND THERE WAS A GREAT CALM—They woke him from his sleep. (He brought peace to others.) (vs 24–26)

6. THERE MET HIM TWO POSSESSED WITH DEVILS (vs 28–33)

IN ONE DAY JESUS SAID YES SIX TIMES AND NO ONLY ONCE!

Matthew 8:17 That it might be fulfilled which was spoken by Esaias the prophet, saying, Himself took our infirmities, and bear *our* sicknesses.

SAYING YES IS ABOUT HELPING OTHERS BEAR THEIR BURDENS.

HERE ARE REASONS TO SAY YES

YOU WILL OVERCOME FEAR AND INSECURITY: THE POWER OF FEAR: Afraid to try new things, afraid to meet new people, afraid of doing anything that might lead to failure. Fear will restrict you, limit you, confine you, and finally paralyze you from moving in God's direction.

One of the greatest reasons most people say "no" is because they are just plain scared and fearful. Fearful to break out of their routine and rut. Fearful of meeting new people. But the more you say "yes," the more you'll face those fears and insecurities head on. And the more you face them, the less intimidating they'll be. Jesus did not say that we would never fear. He said when fear comes, we are to "fear not." Which means that when we experience fear, we are not to respond to it! By saying YES to a fearful situation, the fear of evil loosens its grip of dread it has over you.

MINISTRY DOORS WILL BE OPENED (ACTS 8:26): (Phillip and the Ethiopian eunuch)

Countless opportunities to minister are missed and doors of evangelism are closed simply because we are looking at the earthly circumstances. When Phillip was experiencing great revival, the Holy Spirit spoke and sent him to Gaza, which is a desert place. If he would have paid attention to his natural inclination he would have never gone. It was at this place that Phillip met a powerful Ethiopian spokesman to a queen. He won this man to Christ and the ministry doors were opened. Church history tells us that the Ethiopian helped establish one hundred churches down the Nile River. Wow, now that's a door of ministry!

YOU WILL LEARN SOMETHING NEW: We don't want to break from our routines or try something new for fear of failure or we might look awkward doing it. By trying something new valuable lessons can be learned, even if they don't work. It is obvious that we cannot say yes to everything because we cannot burn the candle at both ends. However, we must realize by saying yes more often than no, we will be opening the door to unlimited possibilities. This will not only help you become the leader of your life but will, without doubt, help you to lead your family and others more effectively.

YOUR GOD CONFIDENCE WILL INCREASE: A powerful peace of mind and heart and an amazing assurance will flood your soul when you decide to say YES.

1. You will boldly move forward with a confidence knowing that God is directing your steps.

2. You will no longer feel the need to correct or control others' behavior or poor choices because you are in control of yourself.

3. You will have a more positive mindset because saying yes puts you on the offense, not the defense.

4. Your relationship guard will be down because you are looking to connect hearts, not close them.

YOU WILL CONNECT WITH & MEET NEW PEOPLE:

PRINCIPLE: "The more people you meet, the more opportunities you will create." You'll get an opportunity to connect with people, meet new people and future friends.

The apostle Paul said in (Galatians 6:10 KJV), "As you therefore have opportunity, do good to all people, especially those who are of the household of faith." Most of the time opportunities are doors opened to meet new people. The scripture says, "Do good." Doing good is a positive attitude and mentality that draws people like a magnetic force to you and to God. It makes you an open door that says, "Welcome." Nothing is more repelling than to arrive at a home that has its blinds drawn, bars on the windows, and a sign that says, "NO SOLICITING." The obvious message it is sending is, "No soliciting, trespassers will be eaten!"

JESUS NEVER STRUGGLED WITH OBEYING GOD, HEALING THE SICK, OR GIVING HIS BEST.

WHY WE SHOULD NOT SAY NO:
OPPORTUNITIES ARE MISSED WHEN WE SAY NO.
CHANGE DOESN'T OCCUR WHEN WE SAY NO.
RELATIONSHIPS ARE NEVER BUILT WHEN WE SAY NO.
PROMISES ARE NOT RECEIVED WHEN WE SAY NO.
POTENTIAL IS NOT RELEASED WHEN WE SAY NO.
NEW THINGS ARE NEVER EXPERIENCED WHEN WE SAY NO.
DREAMS ARE NEVER REALIZED WHEN WE SAY NO.
MINISTRIES ARE NEVER STARTED WHEN WE SAY NO.
MARRIAGES WILL NEVER MATURE OR DEVELOP WHEN WE SAY NO.
GOD IS NOT PURSUED WHEN WE SAY NO.
FEAR IS NEVER DEFEATED WHEN WE SAY NO.

3. IT IS TIME TO PRIORITIZE

Prioritizing helps us to view our daily activities with a right perspective. It also helps us to place them in order of importance. The need for this is priceless because it helps us to keep first things first. The scripture says in (Matthew 6:33 KJV), "But seek ye first the kingdom of God and his righteousness; and all these things shall be added unto you." The previous thirty-two verses, however, deal with the obvious daily needs that all humanity must have met in order to survive, which are food, drink, and clothing.

> The questions we must ask ourselves as leaders in our home are obvious.
> Who will be our source?
> Whom will we trust to meet our needs?
> Whom will we put first?
> The answer can be found in those who lead the home and those who will ultimately make the decisions for their family. Husbands, we must lead from

God's perspective because those that lead from this view will make the right choice.

Whenever my wife and I find ourselves with these immediate needs we ask the same questions. Then we consider our source and whom we will put first. We do not trust in our banks, places of employment, or any other reservoirs to be our source. But, rather, we pray to our Father, which is in heaven, and ask for a heavenly withdrawal. It never ceases to amaze me that within twenty-four hours someone is at our home with a divine deposit. In our marriages and families we must lead by example and show what it really means to trust God.

4. IT IS TIME TO BE INTENTIONAL

Being intentional means to do or act on purpose. It gives the idea of clearly understanding which direction you're headed in and aligning every decision to arrive at your destination. If you do not know where you are headed, you will never arrive at your destination. If you aim at nothing, you will hit it every time. A lot of time can be wasted trying to choose which task is more worthy of your attention. There may be many important challenges that compete for your attention, so which do you choose? When you are uncertain, it causes you to procrastinate or change your mind because you are unclear or confused.

We must understand the principles and truths concerning marriage as outlined in the Bible and base every decision we make with this in view.

WHAT ARE THE STEPS TO INTENTIONAL LIVING?

Intentional living is deliberately taking a step back in order to evaluate w' we are in relation to our goals.

Intentional living is understanding God's plan for ou ually comparing our choices and decisions with God's pla.

Intentional living is viewing our choices in light of eternity.

Intentional living is choosing what is always right though it may cost us dearly.

5. IT IS TIME TO PARTNER WITH GOD

Partnership is simply a binding relationship formed by the agreement between two individuals to carry on a business.

(Corinthians 3:9 AMP) 9 For we are fellow workmen (joint promoters, laborers together] with *and* for God; *you* are God's garden *and* vineyard *and* field under cultivation, [you are] God's building.

PARTNERSHIP IMPLIES...

Having a relationship

Being connected

Going in the same direction

PARTNER IN PRAYER:

(Psalm 5:3 NIV) In the morning, O Lord, you hear my voice; in the morning I lay my requests before you...

WHY PRAY?

Morning signifies three things...

1. Fresh start

2. New opportunities

3. New beginnings

FRESH START: Yesterday is behind us with its burdens, challenges, and ues. God has gifted us with a brand-new day unlike any day that has ever . Prayer and the word give us a fresh perspective and a great attitude life!

Prayer and the word sensitize us and opens our spiritual eyes to see what God sees. Every day God places people in our paths in order for us to impart in prayer what he has deposited within us. This world is lost and hurting and we are the answer to their prayers!

Prayer brings encouragement, cleansing, strength, refreshing, deliverance, and leads to salvation in Christ. Our prayers don't have to be floral or elaborate, just sincere.

NEW OPPORTUNITIES: Prayer helps us keep our priorities in order. The scripture says, "Promotion comes from the Lord." The purpose of a God opportunity is always to advance the kingdom of God. Whether in the form of a new job, a new relationship, a new position, or increased financial blessings, God's intended purpose is for souls to find salvation through Christ through you.

NEW BEGINNINGS: Lastly, prayer gives us discernment and opens our spiritual senses to spiritual things. When God wants to do a new thing in our life, he often will cause a need in our lives to move us toward his perfect will. God sent Elisha to the brook Kidron during a famine to refresh him and feed him through the ravens daily to sustain and bless him for a season.

When God wanted to do something new in his life he dried up the water in the brook and stopped the ravens from delivering food. Elisha was hungry and thirsty. Why would God do this? He had prepared a widow for Elisha to minister to. Rather than complain and gripe, he went to Zapereth where God had commanded the widow to minister to the man of God as he ministered to her. God will place a challenge before us and make us uncomfortable to bring us into a new beginning. So don't complain about your situation; rather, pray and ask the Lord which direction he wants you to go. These are just a few suggestions to better yourself and better your marriage. THE TIME HAS COME!

CHALLENGE:
Go out for coffee and share some humorous stories in your marriage.

TIME TO SUM IT ALL UP!

1. Write one word that summarizes Chapter Three.

2. If you were a counselor, what advice would you give to a struggling couple after you have read Chapter Three?

3. Did you learn anything new?

4. Finish this statement.
When you _____ yourself you automatically _____ your _____.

5. What does it mean to be touchable?

6. What is the Power of Yes?

7. How many times did Jesus say Yes and No in one day?

8. Fill in the blanks.
The more _____ you meet, the more _____ you will create.

9. Why is it important to prioritize?

10. What three things does morning signify?

Chapter Four

THE WATCHPITAL MARRIAGE

Unfortunately a watch doesn't tick forever. We can expect during the duration of its use for there to be repairs needed. I remember once my leather watchband broke partially on one side and was literally hanging by a thread. Rather than repairing it, I wore it anyway, knowing it would not be a problem.

Ladies, I know what you are thinking: typical man. They don't want to ever go to the doctor, ask for directions, or admit when something needs repairing.

Needless to say, whenever I wore it, I was self-conscious, wondering if anyone else noticed. I refused to take it to the watchpital (hospital) to get it repaired. Because of this I didn't look at it much and unbeknownst to me it had lost its beauty and purpose.

So many marriages, like my damaged watch, are hanging by a thread. Their marriages are dull and meaningless, without beauty and purpose also. Those that wear them are afraid to admit that their marriages are in need of repair. In order to avoid our marriages getting to this point, we must constantly monitor the ticking of our marital relationship and tend to the often-needed repairs that only God's word can provide.

CAN I MAKE A SUGGESTION?

EVERY MARRIAGE NEEDS A LITTLE HELP

Quite some time ago I went to a large amusement park. We started at the entrance and went from one section to another. I was amazed how easy it was to get turned around and get lost.

We would enter a ride on one side and exit somewhere else. We would walk a distance to use the restroom and lose our sense of direction when we came out.

We noticed a ride called the "Space Needle." As we boarded it and went to the top we could view the entire park. What seemed so massive and gigantic was now not so intimidating.

We can compare our marriages to the maze of an amusement park. It's easy to get lost if you're not paying attention or get bent out of shape because you are in one section of the park and your spouse in another section.

You want to go to fun-land and your wife wants to go to concert-land. What's the result? Frustration and irritability. Can you see where I am going with this story? We can now compare the "Space Needle" to counseling. The counselor can see the "big picture" and can skillfully guide a couple to safety.

He sees the traps, detours, and the dangers ahead that every marriage experiences. In the book of Acts, 8:26–31, we read the account of Phillip and the Ethiopian Eunuch. The man from Ethiopia was reading the Old Testament scriptures concerning Christ. Philip asked him if he understood what he was reading. Before we look at his response we must consider that this man was a man of wealth and power. His position and pride could have hindered him from responding the way he did. He said, "How can I, except some man should guide me?"

What a wise man! He realized that he needed help. He was willing to admit that he did not know everything and he was ready to receive counsel. Now this is a real man!

This is where so many men get lost. They don't think they need help from anyone. They are too prideful and know too much for their own good. Here's some good advice from (Proverbs 9:9 KJV): "Give instruction to a wise man, and he will be yet wiser: teach a just man, and he will increase in learning."

Counseling also helps us to communicate more effectively because it provides us with a greater understanding of our mate. Always remember this: great communication leads to a greater intimacy. Every aspect of the relationship must be nourished, and nurtured.

Since we have been created tri-part, each aspect of our human experience must find fulfillment. If our marriages are simply based on our sexual experience, our marriages will not last long. There will be no depth or real connection that will be lasting in our relationship. So many marriages base their relationship in this area, therefore it is no great wonder why their marriages do not make it beyond a few years.

Adam and Eve's first connection was a spiritual union that created an in-depth knowing that they were more than flesh. (Genesis 2:23–25 KJV) says, "And Adam said, this *is* now bone of my bones, and flesh of my flesh: she shall be called Woman, because she was taken out of Man. Therefore shall a man leave his father and his mother, and shall cleave unto his wife: and they shall be one flesh. And they were both naked, the man and his wife, and were not ashamed."

THE PROCESS OF A RELATIONSHIP

She shall be called woman because she was taken out of man. The woman was extracted from the inside of the man from the closest place to his heart.

1. There was a spiritual connection first.

Therefore shall a man leave his father and mother, and shall cleave unto his wife: and they shall be one flesh.

2. Here we see the relational aspect of marriage where the husband and wife come together to build a relationship and a kingdom.

Lastly, we read, and they were both naked, the man and his wife, and were not ashamed.

3. Here we see the physical aspect of marriage in the first night in the garden where they consummated the marriage union. Oh what a night!!!!!!

WHAT COUPLE HAS HAD THE GREATEST SEX EVER?

Was it Sonny and Cher?

Was it Mark Antony and Cleopatra?

Was it Bonnie and Clyde?

Was it Brad Pitt and Angelina Jolie?

I submit to you, I believe it was Adam and Eve. Why? There was no manipulation, no jealousy, no anger, no resentment, no unforgiveness, no pride, and no selfishness! Because of this they were able to abandon themselves to one another and be free in their most intimate expressions.

WHAT IS ROMANCE TO A MAN?

RUGGEDNESS: Men love adventure, risk, and conquest in life, especially when it comes to marital love.

REGULARITY: Men love it often, not just when their wives "feel" like it!

RIGHT NOW! Men love it, any time, any place, anywhere, just try me.

WHAT IS ROMANCE TO A WOMAN?

TRUST: When a woman enters a man's domain, she asks the question, "Can I trust you?" Why? Trust deals with vulnerability, submission, and openness.

TIME: This is a marathon, not a forty-yard dash. Women are interested in the journey, not the destination.

TENDERNESS: Women love to be caressed, cuddled, and cared for during the experience.

HOW TO KEEP YOUR MARRIAGE OUT OF THE WATCHPITAL

Now I know I speak for at least 90% of all men in our society. We do not need a physical examination, yearly checkup, or a doctor's appointment. Just leave us alone because whatever ailment is bothering us will go away on its own. Spoken like a true man!

This is not only the way most men approach physical health, but relational health also as it pertains to a vibrant marriage. They simply believe that all of the symptoms of a sickly marriage will work themselves out and go away on their own.

In the forty years that I have been in ministry, 98% percent of the hundreds and hundreds of people that have contacted me for marriage counseling have been the wives, and 2% percent have been the husbands. I have a message for the men reading this book: take care of the early years of your marriage.

When we are young we feel like we are invincible and we will live forever. Eat whatever you want, do whatever you want, and live however you want. But believe me, it will all catch up to you, and payday will come one day!

I never went to the doctors when I was young. I am sixty-two now and last week I went to the hospital seven days in a row. There's an old saying, "Pay me now, or pay me later." What does this mean? We can do the preventative measures now and enjoy the benefits later, or we can wait to do those necessary things and pay the price later in life.

I compare our marriage relationship to a yearly checkup.

What Is A Physical Examination?

1. A physical exam is given to make sure your vitals and overall health are good and to detect if you may possibly have any medical problems that you are unaware of.

2. One of the first things that the doctor will ask about is any medications you are currently taking.

3. The last thing that will be discussed is the physical problems and symptoms you are experiencing to get to the root of the sickness.

Blood Pressure

If it's regularly above normal, your doctor may also order tests to rule out type 2 diabetes. Blood pressure readings have two numbers. For most adults, normal blood pressure is when the top number is less than 120 and the bottom number is less than 80

WHAT CAUSES HIGH BLOOD PRESSURE?

Being overweight. We liken this to having too much of a worldly appetite. *(1 John 2:16 KJV) For everything in the world—the lust of the flesh, the lust of the eyes, and the pride of life—comes not from the Father but from the world."*

It's great for a couple to take inventory in their relationship to make sure their spiritual appearance is balanced and alive.

High blood pressure causes a lack of oxygen to the brain, to the heart, and throughout the body. In order to have a healthy relationship with your spouse, the breath of God must flow through your marriage.

The scripture compares the Holy Spirit to the wind. (Acts 2:2; John 3:8) We must take time to allow the Holy Spirit to breathe the life of the

Father into us. One of the most powerful weapons against the enemy in our marriages is prayer. This is when the wind and breath of God is released to empower and strengthen us as husbands and wives.

I like to use the word picture of a stoplight to illustrate this truth. When the light turns YELLOW it is sending the message to your mind to begin slowing down and concentrate on stopping.

During this phase we remove our minds of all other distractions and begin to focus on Jesus. When we first begin this discipline, our minds will not slow down, but rather continue to race on to all the tasks of our day. As you practice each day, your mind will begin to adjust and automatically make the transition into slow-mo.

The next color the light will turn is RED, which means you must stop and wait for the light to change. This is one of the most important aspects of praying with your spouse. Usually when people are waiting at a stoplight they are anxious, impatient, and irritable. Give me a break; it's only a couple of minutes!

The reason we must learn to wait is because we have too much on our minds, our hearts might not be ready, and, most important, it takes time for the Spirit to prepare our hearts to hear what he is saying to us.

WHAT IS THE ANSWER? Stay On Top of Your Health

In (Matthew 11:28 KJV), the scripture says, "Come unto me all ye that are weary and are heavy laden and I will give you rest. Take my yoke upon you and learn of me for I am meek and lowly of heart and ye shall find rest unto your souls."

I want you to notice 5 truths concerning resting in Christ:

1. We must first COME to Christ to receive His rest.

2. We must ACKNOWLEDGE that the cares of life are too heavy for us to bear alone.

3. Jesus does not force us to rest. He PROVIDES the rest and we enter into it.

4. In order to rest we must be YOKED (connected through fellowship) daily with him.

5. The more we LEARN of His ways, the greater the rest we will experience.

NO OTHER PARTNERS IN BED PLEASE!

Most couples when retiring for a good night's rest do not go to bed alone. They take several other bed partners with them. I know what you're thinking, Pastor, now you're going too far. I'm not talking about people, I'm talking about taking issues as bed partners with us.

So many couples sleep at opposite ends of the bed with a barrel full of conflict, emotional pain, jealousy, and unresolved issues between them. Sleepless nights, tossing and turning throughout the night along with a stomach full of knots.

Rather than a sleep zone, it is a war zone. What should be the most restful time of our day has become the most restless.

WHAT IS THE ANSWER?

(Ephesians 4:26 GW) Be angry without sinning. Don't go to bed angry.

CAN YOU FEEL THE TENSION?

Often, marriage can be hard work, but the benefits far outweigh the issues marriage experiences. As a young pastor in the eighties I had lots of energy to burn. I visited anywhere between seventy-five to a hundred homes a month.

It amazed me, as I went from house to house, the different atmospheres I would sense as I walked into each home. You could feel the anger, resentment, unforgiveness, jealousy, and rage without anyone speaking a word. The tension was so thick you could cut it with a knife. The spiritual, relational, and physical aspects of the home were a feeding frenzy for the enemy. I once knew a couple that was in constant turmoil. If anyone sneezed they were coming down with the flu, if anyone had a stomachache, they had an ulcer, if the car was not in the driveway, it had been stolen. One thing after another, issue after issue.

The hospital had a revolving door with their name on it. There was so much drama, I felt like I was watching a soap opera! The reason I was aware of this was that every time something supposedly went wrong, I received a phone call.

I've learned some things over the years and can give all you couples out there some great truth so you can get off your crazy merry-go-round. Here it is! Issues can be comprised of misunderstandings, resentment, and selfishness. You cannot have a house of peace if you have a relationship where everything is an issue.

Please consider this bit of advice.

MOST ISSUES ARE NOT REALLY ISSUES, JUST DIFFERENT PERSPECTIVES.

A wife may think her husband is being controlling and domineering, not realizing he is acting out of his fixated male perspective. A husband may believe his wife is being disrespectful and rebellious, not realizing she is responding out of her relational perspective.

It is not an issue; it is the way God created the male and female. Don't make it an issue and it won't be an issue. In my household most potential conflicts and issues never arise because my wife and I have learned not to speak them out loud. We let them go like water off a duck's back because we realize that we are only being ourselves.

EXPRESSION MANIFESTS ITSELF IN 3 WAYS

1. Perspective
2. Pleasure
3. Preference

PERSPECTIVE: the viewpoint or angle from which a person sees.

It's a fact that we cannot deny: men's and women's way of looking at life is as different as night and day. God wired them hormonally, psychologically, mentally, and biologically different. She sees the beautiful landscape and vast meadows while driving on a vacation, while he only sees the road in front of him. She wants to hear the experiences and stories, down to the smallest detail when conversing with people. He wants to only know the name and what can you do for me.

What is the conclusion? She wants the experience, he wants to finish. The way that we perceive life is how we respond to it; there is no right or wrong.

PLEASURE: the enjoyment or satisfaction derived from what is to one's liking; delight.

WHAT BRINGS PLEASURE TO A WOMAN

I'd like to give all of you couples out there an acronym to live by. It is the word "WAIT."

W – Give your woman "Worth"

This is giving them value and importance.

A – Give her your "Attention"

We can't fool our wives, because they know whether our focus is on them or not. When she has your attention, she will reward you, and we like to be rewarded!

I – Give her your "Interest"

What is interest? It is the feeling of a person whose attention and concern and curiosity is captured by something. If your wife knows she is your interest and not things, she will respond to you.

T – Let her know she can "Trust" you

This is a great matter for men because broken trust is hard to earn. Men think that women should automatically trust them as the leader and commander. Sorry, trust is earned through relational intercourse. This means that trust is built through intimate talking and intense listening.

WHAT BRINGS PLEASURE TO A MAN

W – Let him know you "Want" him

Every man wants his wife to want him, if you know what I mean!

A – Let them know you "Affirm" them

Every man wants to hear his wife say, "You're the man!"

I – Try to "Initiate" once in a while!

Wanna drive your husband crazy? Chase him around the table, call him to the bedroom, or leave him a love note, "Tonight's the night." It's a guarantee, he will be a better communicator.

T – "Treat" him like a man

No husband likes to be treated like a child. My wife always makes me feel like a success even though I know she is one smart cookie, and a spiritual giant. She always makes me want to take the lead because there can be only one "head" of the home, and she always tells me, "You're a fine specimen of a man!"

THINK ABOUT IT

For the man, the acronym for "wait" is sexual, and for the woman it is relational.

In all actuality there is no conflict or issue, just a different perspective and preference that will consummate in pleasure!

WHAT IS THE ANSWER?

Respect the difference. When we realize that God created men and women different in every fashion, we can gain an insight into how to relate to them. Men and women problem-solve, think, talk, and feel differently as they see life.

WHEN WE RESPECT THE DIFFERENCE, WE CAN CELEBRATE THE DIFFERENCE.

The best part of a team is that when one scores all can celebrate. Most married couples act as though their spouses are on the opposing team. No, we are on the same team. The key here is to begin to cooperate with our mate, accept their creativity, perspective, and gifts they bring to the team. In doing this we can assure we are on the same team, going in the same direction. Because if we never score we can never celebrate, and I like to celebrate!

PREFERENCE: what a person likes or prefers.

Mostly we develop preferences from our upbringing and simply the manner in which our family functioned, the places we visited, the things we ate, the vacations we enjoyed, and the types of people we associated with.

The scripture solidifies this truth in (Proverbs 22:6 KJV): "6 Train up a child in the way he should go: and when he is old, he will not depart from it."

The root word for train means, "Putting something in the mouth." The meaning of the word is "bending a twig in a specific direction."

The combination of these two meanings implies "Nourishment and deliberately pointing in a certain direction." That's why when a couple first starts in a relationship you really cannot see who they actually are. It is buried deep behind the mask they wear and takes time to surface. Most couples when dating don't really care what places they visit because they just want to be with him/her. However, as time passes in the relationship, all that begins to change and that's when the fun begins! One thing about marriage is as the years pass by, you either blend together or grow apart.

Some aspects in marriage that we must pay attention to are…

1. STAYING CONNECTED WITH YOUR WIFE
2. NOT IGNORING HER SENSITIVITY
3. NOT ALWAYS LEAVING HER ALONE
4. NOT ALWAYS BEING SILENT

It's a fact that one of the essential lifelines and greatest needs of a woman is to connect with others. The need to relate and interact with others cannot be ignored; it must be met in order for her to be fulfilled and complete.

CHALLENGE:

Using the acronym, "W-A-I-T," talk about various ways each of you could begin applying this advice.

TIME TO SUM IT ALL UP!

1. Write one word that summarizes Chapter Four.

2. If you were a counselor, what advice would you give to a struggling couple after you read Chapter Four?

3. Did you learn anything new?

4. Why is counseling so vital for a married couple?

5. What is the process of a relationship?

6. What are the 3 ways that expression is manifested?

7. Fill in the blanks.
When we _____ the difference, we can _____ the difference.

8. What does the acronym "Wait" for a woman stand for?

9. What does the acronym "Wait" for a man stand for?

Chapter Five

DON'T THROW IT AWAY!

Over the years I have purchased and received some pretty amazing watches. When I removed it from its' case, it seemed so perfect and flawless. And then it happened! I bumped it against the side of a wall and scratched the face. I removed it from the box and dropped it, and when I took a dip in the pool, I forgot to take it off! Then my first thought was to discard it and throw it away. The only problem was, it's still ticking, useful, and serving its purpose.

People have a lot in common with these damaged goods. During the process of everyday living, people are bumped, dropped, scraped, battered, cracked, and just plain abused! The world has a way of dishing out pain and sorrow to everyone. Don't let anyone fool you, because everyone has experienced rejection, failures, disappointments, and their fair share of losses.

Most of the time when two people meet and begin forming a relationship their issues are deep-seated and hidden behind a great acting performance and a smiling face. But like the Lone Ranger, Iron Man, Batman, and Cat woman, the mask has to come off sooner or later, and when it does you will discover that they are average, ordinary people, flaws and all, just like you and me. The truth is, there are no knights in shining armor, no superheroes, and, I'm sorry to burst your bubble, there are no sleeping beauties. Only those beauties who wake up in curlers and have bad breath! When we first meet a person it all seems so magical and perfect. Right! My advice to anyone who is rushing into a relationship is, hold your horses, put on the brakes, and let the real person come out.

I'm not discouraging anyone from entering into a relationship, nor am I implying that you have to wait decades to make sure. I am simply stating the truth revealed in scripture. (Genesis 1:28 KJV) And God blessed them, and God said unto them, Be fruitful, and multiply, and replenish the earth, and subdue it: and have dominion over the fish of the sea, and over the fowl of the air, and over every living thing that moveth upon the earth.

Please understand this: "Marriage is not a heavenly institution, but an earthly institution." With all its flaws and misunderstandings, with all its imperfections and attitudes. I have counseled enough naïve young couples that believe that their relationship would never have any issues or arguments. Boy, were they surprised! I am not a negative person, just someone who understands that people are broken, wounded, bruised, and emotionally battered. Everyone on planet Earth has experienced criticism, rejection, hurt, and pain.

MY SAD STORY

Where I am now, as a pastor and an author, is truly a miracle. My education from elementary through high school was one continuous nightmare. It all began one morning in fourth grade when my teacher pointed to me and asked a question. She told me to stand and give the answer. There I stood with all eyes on me and the spotlight of the world shining in my face. Of course I did not know the answer, so I just shrugged my shoulders and nodded my head. The teacher replied, "What are you, stupid?" Like I had a stake through my heart, I began to bleed emotionally.

For the next three years my teachers hit me, slapped me, and pulled my hair. What do you do when you are bullied by your own teachers? If I was bullied by a classmate, I could tell the principal or a teacher. I could tell my parents, but would they believe me? So I simply took the abuse! Names such as stupid, idiot, and ugly were the message laid on the shoulders of a little boy who was too small to fight back.

What did I learn during the elementary school years? Absolutely nothing! I became a silent casualty of the corrupt school system that just pushed me through each grade with a straight-F average. By the time I reached junior high I realized that the only way to escape any more abuse was to fight back, and fight back is exactly what I did! I fought with classmates, students from other schools, teachers, principals, and anyone else that challenged me. I cut school for days, weeks, and months at a time trying to escape my personal hell.

What kept me in school was a little cutie I met in ninth grade, Marilyn Dawn Sabo. She was bright, enthusiastic, intelligent and beautiful. She was everything I wasn't and she had a way of making me feel that I could find success also. She never put me down or made me feel inferior; most of all, she accepted me for who I was.

What did I learn in my junior-high and high-school days? Absolutely nothing! Every time I went to class it felt like a prison. Every paper handed to me was thrown away and every question asked was met with vulgarity and violence.

THE TURNAROUND

When I was twelve years old I had tons of friends in our neighborhood. One in particular was Jim Lightfoot. His father was pastor at a Korean Baptist church where all they talked about was Jesus. One day we sat together in my bedroom where he introduced me to the Savior. Now I can say with confidence that Jesus was there all the time. A few years would pass when Marilyn would find the Savior and one year later reintroduce me to him, also.

From that point on, my life began to change drastically. I began to learn, grow, and flourish in every area of my life. God began to open doors of opportunity by connecting me with people who would be able to advance me in life. A scripture revealed this principle to me, found in (Galatians 6:10

NKJV): "Therefore, as we have opportunity, let us do good to all, especially to those who are of the household of faith."

The principle is this: "The more people you meet, the more opportunities you will create." Every person in life has influence, connections, and relationships, which God uses to advance us in life. Jesus Himself, according to the scripture, lived his life by this same principle. (Luke 2:52 KJV) And Jesus increased in wisdom and stature, and in favour with God and man.

We must understand that God uses people to advance us in life. There are two truths revealed in this scripture text.

1. Wisdom and strength comes from God.
2. God blesses people through people.

Prior to rededicating my life to Christ, I found it difficult to receive encouraging and affirming words. This was due to receiving the negative messages from a society who viewed a young man as not having any worth or significance.

Every time that I made an attempt to accomplish a task or try something new I was met with the distant voices of the past who spoke loud and clear. Failure. Stupid. Why even try? Nobody believes in you and everyone knows how ignorant you really are! What was the result of the barrage of insults and painful memories? I was fearful to learn, fearful to try anything, and fearful to reveal to anyone who I actually was.

When I rededicated my life to Christ at the age of twenty-one, I was skeptical of believing that someone could love me and care for me exactly how I was. Why would anyone choose to put any value or worth in someone who failed constantly and had nothing to offer? There were two scriptures that I discovered that can heal any person and any relationship.

(John 3:16–17 KJV) 16 For God so loved the world, that he gave his only begotten Son, that whosoever believeth in him should not perish, but have everlasting life. 17 For God sent not his Son into the world to condemn the world; but that the world through him might be saved.

When we understand that every person has issues, hurts, pain, and failures, we can become a part of the solution rather than part of the pain.

1. FOR GOD SO LOVED

God's love is a choice that he makes to bestow his amazing agape love upon those who do not deserve it. It is based solely upon the one who chooses to love. When we choose to love with God's love there is no expectation or stipulations attached to it. It is freely given with no hidden agenda. If most married couples would operate in this principle their marriages would be happier and healthier.

2. THAT HE GAVE

There is a price to be paid when we choose to love. God's choice to love cost the life of His One and Only Son. To love is to give, and to give is a sacrifice, and a sacrifice is to pay the price for someone else's freedom.

3. THAT WHOSOEVER BELIEVETH IN HIM

The husband or wife who chooses to be the first to ask forgiveness, the one who seeks to do the right thing, or the one who seeks to reconcile is the one who pays the price. In our relationship with God, he says, "Put the weight on me and I will see us through." It takes a person of courage and confidence, and a person of spiritual fortitude and humility, to exhibit this type of character.

4. SHOULD NOT PERISH

What Does it Mean to "Perish?"

Whenever you see Jesus use a word such as "**perish**" or "destroy," the original word is "apollumi." The **Greek** word "apollumi" means "to lose, or to be lost."

When a couple seeks to save their marriage they must have the focus and attitude of God. In order for our marriage not to perish we must keep it front and center. This means we must first choose to love our mate no matter what. Secondly, we must manifest our love through unselfishly giving, to minister the genuine love of God to our companion. Most couples abandon their marriages because they have lost their love. My advice to those couples is this: "If you have lost your first love, then you can find it once again." How do you accomplish this?

    a. You must view your marriage as priceless and precious.

    b. You just need to know where to look!

5. FOR GOD SENT NOT HIS SON TO CONDEMN THE WORLD. BUT THAT THE WORLD THROUGH HIM MIGHT BE SAVED.

The last challenge we must accept is this: we must become the savior of our marriage. What is the savior's duty? He is to do all that he can to restore, resurrect, and save his marriage. His attitude must be, I will never quit, never walk away, and even be willing to give my life to save it. Most troubled couples give up too easily and too soon.

Can you imagine if Jesus had this attitude? He would have ascended back to heaven in a flash. No, he stayed because he loved us too much and was willing to fight to win us back to himself.

The scripture says in (Luke 19:10 KJV), "For the Son of man is come to seek and to save that which was lost." Our Lord's purpose for seeking is to save, period! He is determined, single-minded, and wanting to fully restore us to himself! Luke 2:9 (KJV) says, "And I say unto you, Ask, and it shall be given you; seek, and ye shall find; knock, and it shall be opened unto you."

Many have understood this scripture to mean that whatever you ask for in prayer, God will grant it. This could not be further from the truth, because many of the things people ask for are for selfish reasons, with wrong motives and prideful intentions.

The first question we must ask concerning this scripture when in prayer is, what are we to ask for? The answer is obvious: we are to ask for the same thing our Lord asked for, salvation, reuniting, and broken fellowship restored. When we seek with a sincere heart we always get the right results. The scripture ends with the believer standing before their God door. It indicates that every time they knock on this door, it will open, every time. Why? Because if every married couple had this mindset I believe there would be fewer couples in divorce court and more and more happy marriages. Your marriage is worth fighting for and dying for! It's all about how much you value your mate. So don't throw it away; give it to the Marriage Maker!

STRAIGHT FROM THE HORSE'S MOUTH

As we age, aches and pains are a normal part of life that affect us all sooner or later. What are the contributors to sore muscles and joint pain? Yardwork, bike riding, cleaning the garage, changing a flat tire, chasing a two-year-old for six hours, playing football, tennis, or going to the gym. One thing about these sore muscles is they certainly slow us down and make us immobile for a few days. What is the answer? Sore muscle cream! Bengay, Aspercream, Tiger Balm, OxyRub, Biofreeze, Sports Cream, Mineral Ice, and the list goes on. I've personally tried a few of these products and they all worked!

However, as the years roll by, my aches, pains, and soreness last a little longer, and I am constantly reminded by the many advertisements in my mailbox that I am reaching my golden years! AARP, convalescent homes, senior-living brochures, retirement information, and the other day I received information on burial insurance. Wait a minute, I'm still warm!

That's why I love being around young people. They are lively, reckless, enthusiastic, spontaneous, and mobile. Their conversations start off with challenges and end with adventure. They are fearless, unpredictable, and sometimes a little scary! If you think you're getting a little old, here's some humor for you.

YOU KNOW YOU'RE OLD WHEN...

1. Your little black book only has the phone numbers of your pharmacist and doctors.
2. The old lady you help cross the street is your wife.
3. Your back goes out more than you do.
4. You sing along with the music in the elevator.
5. All you watch on TV is PBS.
6. You have more hair in your ears than on your head.
7. Everything in your grocery cart says "for fast relief."
8. Getting lucky means finding your car in the parking lot.

I always advise people that do not have any excitement in their life and believe they are growing old to rent a kid, borrow a kid, or just invite your sister's kids over for an afternoon. Kids bring life, excitement, and joy to any home.

The church that I pastor is full of young people and lots of kids. The reason I love it is because it makes me feel young when I am surrounded by them. Now, I did not say look young because it is not a cure for your wrinkles or crow's feet, but it makes you feel energetic and young at heart.

One day I called my brother Darren, and during our conversation my aches and pains came up. He said, "Have I got something for you!" A few days later he shows up at my house with a white bottle that said "sore muscles and joint pain relief."

However, in bold letters it was labeled "Veterinary Liniment." And to top it all off it had a picture with a horse on it! I said, "You want me to put this on me or my dog?" He said they use it on horses and at the convalescent home. Now that's where I draw the line! I'm sixty-one, but I am not ready for the old-folks home, right?

Then I remembered my conversation for the last three years; you know, the conversation when those over sixty sit around and see who can top each other's stories of aches, pains, and varicose veins. When I get together with my friends, I tell them I hurt, here, here, and here. How about you? Oh no! I've become an old zombie! Needless to say, I tried the horse liniment and boy did it work! When I applied it, it seemed to go down to my outer muscles, inner muscles, joints, and straight down to the bones. All I can say is, "Try it, you'll like it!"

Like the horse liniment, the word of God is the best remedy around for those marriages that experience the deep pains of life. Why go anywhere else once we find out what really works and what can bring relief to a troubled marriage?

(Hebrews 4:12 AMP) For the word of God is living and active *and* full of power [making it operative, energizing, and effective]. It is sharper than any two-edged [a]sword, penetrating as far as the division of the [b]soul and spirit [the completeness of a person], and of both joints and marrow [the deepest parts of our nature], exposing *and* judging the very thoughts and intentions of the heart.

5 THINGS GOD'S WORD BRINGS IN A MARRIAGE

Life – Power – Energy - Ministering to our soul and spirit - Reveals our thoughts to bring emotional healing

So don't throw your marriage away; just let God's word revive, renew, and restore it for a lifetime.

CHALLENGE: Share a time in your life when you were disappointed or hurt. End your talk by praying for each other.

TIME TO SUM IT ALL UP!

1. Write one word that summarizes Chapter Five.

2. If you were a counselor, what advice would you give to a struggling couple after you have read Chapter Five?

3. Did you learn anything new?

4. True or false?

    Sharing God's love is a choice. True ( ) False ( )

    There is a price to be paid when we choose to love. True ( ) False ( )

    It takes a coward to ask for forgiveness. True ( ) False ( )

    We must manifest God's love through selfishness. True ( ) False ( )

5. Fill in the blanks.

    Most troubled couples give up to _____ and to _____.

6. What is the Savior's duty?

7. What are we to ask for in prayer?

8. Fill in the blanks.
Your marriage is worth _____ for and _____ for.

9. What are 6 things God's word brings in a marriage?

Chapter Six

TAKES A LICKING AND KEEPS ON TICKING

Remember the commercial? Their watches were marketed not for their elegance or beauty but for their durability. The commercial presented a watch being struck at point-blank range by a bow and arrow. The next test, they fastened the watch to a motorboat propeller, immersed it in water, and then turned it on! What was the commercial message? Do what you can to stop it from working, but it will keep doing what it was created to do, keep on ticking!

KID-PROOF

Have you ever noticed the toughness and guts of children? They get slammed, bashed, thrown, bounced, hit, whipped, and crushed, then five minutes later they are back at it again. Why? They are kid-proof! When something is kid-proof, it has been proven, tested, tried, and spent, to find out if it has what it takes. Takes a licking and keeps on ticking! Remember the old toy the Weebles? Weebles wobble, but they don't fall down. They just keep getting right back up and start all over again.

When my kids were little, they would rush into the house at least five times a day, crying, screaming, and bleeding! Josh pushed me off the fence. Ben hit me in the head with a rock. Abe just jumped off the roof. My all-time favorite was when Ben and Josh built a ramp. Ben went over face first and embedded his two front teeth into the concrete!

Similarly, marriage was created to last a lifetime. Throughout the centuries and ages, society and humanistic thinking has sought to change, redefine, and destroy God's original purpose and intent concerning marriage. Let's not forget who created, instituted, and established marriage. It was God! He is the Marriage Maker and He has the last word! The enemy of all that is righteous and holy has attempted to annihilate and destroy God's blessed union, but as with everything else that God has initiated, God will prevail!

THERE'S A SNAKE IN MY GARDEN!

We once had some parishioners in our church named Brother and Sister Pope. They lived in a tri-level home nestled on twenty acres. One morning Sister Pope was working in her garden, digging and planting. As she reached her hand under a leafy plant she heard the most terrifying noise. It was hidden where it could not be seen, but by its distinctive sound, she knew exactly what it was, a poisonous rattlesnake! As fast as she could, she drew her hand back and leaped to her feet. Close call avoided!

HIDDEN IN YOUR PARADISE

In the beautiful garden paradise that God had prepared for the first couple, everything was perfect. Lush green meadows, cascading waterfalls, indescribable flowers and vegetation as far as the eye could see. It was truly heaven on earth. However, during their garden tour, God pointed to a forbidden area. Let's read.

(Genesis 2:16–17 KJV) 16 And the LORD God commanded the man, saying, Of every tree of the garden thou mayest freely eat: 17 But of the tree of the knowledge of good and evil, thou shalt not eat of it: for in the day that thou eatest thereof thou shalt surely die.

What always amazes me every time I read this story is that Adam and Eve had it all. They were blessed beyond measure, they had more than anyone could desire, but somehow it was not enough. Notice that Eve was nowhere to be found when God gave these instructions. She had not yet been created, which means that Adam was the only one given these guidelines and warnings. It was his responsibility to pass the information on to Eve.

In (Genesis 3:1 KJV), it explicitly says, "Now the serpent was more subtil than any beast of the field which the LORD God had made."

I am thoroughly convinced that God did not leave any doubt of the danger and consequence of this particular tree. I can hear God's voice as I take a little liberty with the scriptural account. "I know that the tree seems absolutely harmless and innocent; however, cowering and twisted around it is a deceptive, beguiling serpent who will twist and distort my truth."

Apparently, it was not clear enough to Adam what God meant when he said, "of the tree of the knowledge of good and evil, thou shall not eat thereof." I believe when God was warning them he was pointing at the tree from a distance.

When I was in the construction industry we often worked around very dangerous environments. Several times the electricians would leave the door open of a live power box loaded with thousands of volts of electricity. If you placed your hand in the wrong place it would definitely be a one-way ticket to meet Jesus face to face. Therefore, they would place caution tape, toolboxes, warning signs, barricades, and anything else to detour and stop anyone from getting within fifteen feet of this deadly hazard. Get the picture!

If you know anything about washing clothes, you are aware that every garment has a warning label on it pertaining to its care. Some may say wash with like color clothes, only use non-chlorine bleach, wash with delicates, hang dry, or dry clean only. The warnings are given for a reason. One day I decided to wash all my white undies with one pair of Marilyn's pink socks, and I walked around for a few months wearing pick underwear. Lesson learned! When you ignore and avoid the warning signs, you pay the consequences.

I believe that the tree of the knowledge of good and evil was not a dried, parched, lifeless, and undesirable tree but a beautiful tree. Basically, it appeared harmless, but like the thousand-volt electrical box, it would leave you graveyard dead!

When God spoke to Adam and Eve, he implied, keep your distance, don't go near it, and don't even look in that direction, stay away. The only problem with this tree was it was a talking tree! Hidden deep within its branches and leaves was a beguiling serpent, a deadly poisonous snake waiting to strike.

I can imagine as Eve would pass by from a distance he would call out to her, "Hey, Eve, how are you? Beautiful day we're having, isn't it?" His voice did not sound evil or threatening. As a matter of fact it sounded more like a friend or an acquaintance. Then, little by little and day by day, she came closer and closer, until she came face to face with Satan himself.

The next step to Satan's plan was to get Eve close enough to whisper in her ear.

(Genesis 3:1–6 KJV)

1 And he said unto the woman, Yea, hath God said, Ye shall not eat of every tree of the garden?

2 And the woman said unto the serpent, We may eat of the fruit of the trees of the garden:

3 But of the fruit of the tree which *is* in the midst of the garden, God hath said, Ye shall not eat of it, neither shall ye touch it, lest ye die.

4 And the serpent said unto the woman, Ye shall not surely die:

5 For God doth know that in the day ye eat thereof, then your eyes shall be opened, and ye shall be as gods, knowing good and evil.

6 And when the woman saw that the tree *was* good for food, and that it *was* pleasant to the eyes, and a tree to be desired to make *one* wise, she took of the fruit thereof, and did eat.

Here, Satan was close enough to coil around Eve, so he went for the jugular. He appealed to her fleshly appetite, her natural eyes, and her prideful intellect. This scenario would have never happened if she would have kept her distance and took heed of the warning clearly outlined by God. The real danger for any married couple is when you get close enough to have a conversation with Satan. It is at this point where he can inject doubt, and challenge God's covenant. My advice to anyone is ignore the enemy and don't even give him the time of day.

As a married couple, don't be fooled at all. Satan is after your marriage and your soul. Just ask the millions of couples who have crossed the line and disregarded the warnings in the word of God. Unfaithfulness, abuse, divorce, unforgiveness, lying, neglect, lack of marital prayer, disrespect, and lost love. If they could do it all over, they would have guarded, cherished, cared, and focused on God and their marriage. What is the message? Keep your distance from the areas that God's word says will kill your marriage.

SILENT DEATH

Someone has said that "silence is golden." I suppose it is when a stay-at-home mom has dealt with her screaming children pulling on her apron all day, or a construction worker has listened to the pounding of machinery for eight hours. At the end of the day, all we want is peace and quiet. This type of silence can be rejuvenating, restful, and life-giving. However, there is a silence in our nation that has disabled and crippled the marriages throughout our nation. It is called "Silent Authority."

The scripture may have implied that each time Eve conversed with the serpent she was alone, but when you take a closer look at the text it reveals a different story.

(Genesis 3:6–7 KJV)

6 And when the woman saw that the tree *was* good for food, and that it *was* pleasant to the eyes, and a tree to be desired to make *one* wise, she took of the fruit thereof, and did eat, and gave also unto her husband with her; and he did eat.

7 And the eyes of them both were opened, and they knew that they *were* naked;

The truth is that Adam was present each time Eve encountered the serpent. I'm not certain if he was intimidated by the serpent or if he wanted Eve to take the lead. Typical woman; she didn't have anyone to talk to, so she talked to the serpent. Typical man; choosing to be silent and watch TV. Whatever the case, he chose not to speak up and take his place in God's divine order. No doubt about it, Adam's silence was the influence behind Eve's disobedience. It was his duty and responsibility to defend his home, speak up, and take authority over the enemy. He not only lost his spiritual life that day, he lost his influence over and respect of his precious wife!

This familiar story is the reason our nation is deteriorating before our very eyes. Men who would rather be a follower than a leader in their home. Men that would spend their energy on hobbies and other interests rather than placing their energy and heart into the salvation of their family. Men who hide behind a skirt and let the wife lead in spiritual matters concerning the family. Where are the men who are willing to pay the price, against all odds, and say with Joshua, "As for me and my house, we will serve the Lord."

DO YOU LOVE THE DARK?

When we were kids my parents took us on a tour to Alcatraz Island. When we arrived we hopped off the boat for some exploration and adventure. It was a gorgeous summer day, the sun was shining bright and clear, and we were ready for some fun.

Our tour guide led us to the yard where the inmates use to exercise. We went to the mess hall, the library, and even viewed all the floors with the jail cells. My brothers and sisters laughed, played, and goofed around the entire time during the tour. The last area our guide would take us was called solitary confinement. Solitary confinement is the practice of isolating people in closed cells for twenty-two to twenty-four hours a day, virtually free of human contact, for periods of time ranging from days to decades. As we walked down a long corridor a holy hush came over our entire group. Without one word spoken we all realized that in days past, this was where they housed the most notorious and violent criminals on this lonely island.

There were about twenty people in our tour as they escorted us one by one into this iron-plated cell. All we sensed in this room was a darkness that sent chills up our spines and a gloominess that reached out and enveloped you with its tentacles. Then, all of a sudden, the door shut with the sound of hopeless imprisonment, as the darkness swallowed us into a place of nothingness. It was so dark you could not even see your hand in front of your face.

Even though the cell was full of people, the darkness made you feel like you were all alone. Your senses attempted to compensate in this gross darkness, but the deep darkness seemed to swallow up any hope while fear and dread took its place. This brings me to my next point. This is why Satan loves the darkness, because he is revealed in scripture as the prince of darkness. The "Prince of Darkness" (Ephesians 6:12 KJV) is a term that means the he is the embodiment of evil. Satan works, plans, operates, and lives in the darkness.

The scripture says in (John 3:19–21 NKJV) "19 And this is the condemnation, that the light has come into the world, and men loved darkness rather than light, because their deeds were evil. 20 For everyone practicing evil hates the light and does not come to the light, lest his deeds should be exposed. 21 But he who does the truth comes to the light, that deeds may be clearly seen, that they have been done in God."

What does this mean? The only way that Satan can work in your life and in your marriage is if you give him a place to hide. Therefore it is vital that a marriage be based upon honesty, openness, and transparency. My wife and I always make a point to let each other know what we are going through and how we can help and support each other.

When Adam and Eve were in the garden it said that they "walked with God," which implies that they journeyed with God as they shared life's experiences together.

I want you to notice five things about the darkness.

1. **Light is greater than darkness.** One great illustration is this: Have you ever seen the darkness pierce the light? No; it is scientifically impossible for the darkness to pierce the light. However, if you squeeze into a refrigerator box and seal yourself in, then punch a hole in the side of the box, light will stream in and conquer the darkness.
2. **We must keep our hearts filled with the light of God's word, because darkness will try to lure us and pull us in.**
3. **In God there is no darkness at all.**
4. **We expose the deeds of darkness by God's presence and God's word.**
5. **God's power is manifested in your life by the light (truth).**

This implies that as a married couple, we must keep our relationship open. No secrets, white lies, and hidden agendas. Your marriage can be blessed and last a lifetime if you will remain transparent and open to God, the Marriage Maker!

CHALLENGE:

Take a walk together and share some practical steps each of you could begin to implement to guard your marriage relationship.

TIME TO SUM IT ALL UP!

1. Write one word that summarizes Chapter Six.

2. If you were a counselor, what advice would you give to a struggling couple after you have read Chapter Six?

3. Did you learn anything new?

4. True or false?
   God created marriage to last a lifetime. True ( ) False ( )
   God failed to warn Adam and Eve about the serpent. True ( ) False ( )

5. What did the enemy appeal to when tempting Eve?

6. How did Satan inject doubt and challenge God's covenant?

7. Fill in the blanks.
The real danger for any married couple is when you get _____ enough to have a _____ with Satan.

8. True or false?
Adam was not present each time Eve encountered the serpent.
   True ( ) False ( )
Adam's silence was the influence behind Eve's disobedience.
   True ( ) False ( )

9. It was Adam's duty and responsibility to _____ the home, _____, and take _____ over the enemy.

10. Where does Satan love to hide in a marriage?

Chapter Seven

TIME TO CHOOSE WISELY

SIX WAYS TO MAKE WISE CHOICES

WE MAKE THOUSANDS OF CHOICES and decisions on a daily basis. I don't believe any married couple wakes up each morning with the intent of making wrong decisions. However, often our emotions get the best of us as we stray from using common sense and damage our relationship through bad behavior. This chapter will give us helpful guidelines and rules from the Book of Proverbs that we can apply that can help in growing a healthy relationship.

PROVERBS

A GOOD DEFINITION is "short sentences that present practical truth for prosperous, godly living." The word *proverb* means "to be like"; therefore, the book of Proverbs is a book of comparisons leading us in making wise, every day, common choices.

The purpose of a proverb is to reveal hidden wisdom in a short, bite-size, memorable sentence. Proverbs are simplistic yet profound.

PROVERBS ARE SHORT SENTENCES THAT HAVE BEEN LIVED OUT FROM LONG EXPERIENCES.

We are constantly reminded in Proverbs to…

SEEK WISDOM

GET WISDOM

UNDERSTAND WISDOM

Purpose of Writing: Knowledge versus wisdom.

Knowledge is the gathering of facts or learning of information, but wisdom is knowledge and good judgment based on experience. Wisdom is seeing what God sees, and then applying its truth to my situation. I believe that the book of Proverbs is the best how-to book ever written, because its common-sense advice, if applied, will bring wealth, peace, health, righteousness, and contentment in this life that will lead to life eternal.

In the Book of Proverbs, Solomon reveals the wisdom and mind of God that is heavenly and applies them in ordinary, everyday experiences. Unlike the other books in the Bible, the Book of Proverbs can be challenging to summarize. It is wisdom and wisdom alone that is found throughout the pages of this treasured book. Why? First, there are no obvious individuals or persons presented in the book. Second, it is difficult because there is no actual storyline either.

May I give you a few suggestions for how to make wise choices as a married couple?

1. Don't make choices too quickly.

(Proverbs 18:13 KJV) He that answereth a matter before he heareth it, it is folly and shame unto him.

(Proverbs 18:13 CEV) It's stupid and embarrassing to give an answer before you listen.

What does this mean? Don't be in a hurry when making an important decision, when the outcome will not only affect you but those around you. Think before you speak, act, or choose. Let time and space be your ally and not your enemy. There is a cost to every decision that we make; therefore, learning to first wait on God, or asking for the godly counsel of others, we can avoid making a wrong choice. If we want to grow and mature as a couple, we must practice this great piece of advice.

2. Don't make choices without consulting God.

(Proverbs 16:1–3 GNT) 1 We may make our plans, but God has the last word. 2 You may think everything you do is right, but the LORD JUDGES YOUR MOTIVES. 3 Ask the LORD TO BLESS YOUR PLANS, AND YOU WILL BE SUCCESSFUL IN CARRYING THEM OUT.

What does a consultant do?

Consultants are individuals that assist us and share their expertise in personal and business matters to help solve difficult problems and reach our goals. Where can we find a greater consultant than God Himself? After all, He created, fashioned, and instituted marriage, so why go anywhere else to find out "how to" do marriage?

God gave us the word of God because it is a book about vertical and horizontal relationships. The scripture records in the book of (Matthew 27:50–51 KJV), "50 Jesus, when he had cried again with a loud voice, yielded up the ghost. 51 And, behold, the veil of the temple was rent in twain from the top to the bottom; and the earth did quake, and the rocks rent."

The veil was torn by God Himself, revealing that God had pulled down every barrier between God and man through the offering of his Son upon the cross. The scripture encourages us to come with boldness and confidence before His throne to receive grace in our situation. The Lord has all the answers to our relational difficulties and is ready to give us instruction and wisdom out of His word. It is God's great desire for us as a married couple to have a vertical relationship with him as we come to him with our daily needs and challenges.

The next scripture is found in (Ephesians 2:14 NIV): "For he himself is our peace, who has made the two groups one and has destroyed the barrier, the dividing wall of hostility."

What does this mean? God, through Christ, has removed the wall between God and man. We can be reassured that as we consult God in the matters of marital relationships he can bring the peace that we so desperately need.

3. Don't make choices to follow the crowd.

(Proverbs 1:10, 14–15 KJV) 10 My son, if sinners entice thee, consent thou not. 14 Cast in thy lot among us; let us all have one purse: 15 My son, walk not thou in the way with them; refrain thy foot from their path.

Basically this scripture is warning us as a married couple to…

1. Not be influenced by the world

The systems and standards of the world have lost their sense of direction concerning marriage. Marriage to our society is nothing more than a piece of paper that can be ripped up and discarded. When we take the advice of the world it can affect our mindset and in our relationship with our significant other, where they no longer are significant.

2. Not play by the rules of the world

Actually, the world doesn't have rules concerning marital behavior. It is rather an "anything goes" attitude and way of thinking. The world believes that the reward is worth the risk when it comes to breaking their marriage vows.

3. Not become an influencer like the world

(Psalm 1:1 NIV) Blessed is the one who does not walk in step with the wicked or stand in the way that sinners take or sit in the company of mockers.

This scripture gives a three-step warning. 1. Do not be influenced by the advice of those who do not follow Christ. 2. Do not pattern your life after them. 3. Do not influence others to follow the ways of the world concerning marriage.

The steps are, we become…

1. Influenced
2. Impacted
3. Influencer

Those things that we said we would never do become a way of living to us!

4. Don't make choices with your guard down.

(Proverbs 4:23 KJV) Keep thy heart with all diligence; for out of it *are* the issues of life.

If you know anything about the sport of boxing, you know it is dangerous to enter the ring with your guard down. Any contestant making this decision will wake up tomorrow morning with an Excedrin headache!

There is a reason we are commanded to keep our guard up.

When our guard is down we are persuaded to lower our standards concerning our marital morals. Keeping our guard up implies…

- We keep our guard up because we value our marriage union as God's precious treasure to us.
- We place barriers and borders around our marriage relationship to guard against temptation and infidelity.
- We keep our guard up because we don't want to suffer the damage and consequences of a broken marriage.

(1 Thessalonians 5:6–7 KJV) 6 Therefore let us not sleep, as *do* others; but let us watch and be sober.

7 For they that sleep sleep in the night; and they that be drunken be drunken in the night.

In the long run you will be glad because you took the precaution to keep your guard up and keep the enemy out of your marriage.

5. Don't make choices when angry.

(Proverbs 16:32 AMP) He who is slow to anger is better *and* more honorable than the mighty [soldier], And he who rules *and* controls his own spirit, than he who captures a city.

WHAT HAPPENS TO US BIOLOGICALLY WHEN WE GET ANGRY?

Usually, we all make the wrong decisions when we are mad. It begins in our brains when we are undisciplined in our emotions. The amygdala, located in the frontal lobe in the brain, is the decision-making faculty, where rational thinking and behavior is lived out. The moment that the emotion of anger is triggered the blood in our bodies attack this area. When this occurs all logic and reasoning fly out the window.

The next step is affecting our adrenal glands, producing anxiety, stress, and pressure that heighten our energy and blood pressure and heart rate.

At this point it is difficult to think clearly because your anger is almost out of control. Talk about making a mountain out of a molehill, overreacting, and blowing the issue out of perspective; you've just crossed the line of no return.

The emotion of anger is a God-given emotion. However, it is only useful in protecting yourself in life-and-death situations or defending God's righteous cause. The Bible encourages us to turn from your anger, not let it turn into sin, and not go to bed with it. So the next time you start to make a decision when you're angry, stop, think, count to ten, and wait in prayer. Did you know that prayer affects your brain?

6. Don't make the choice to follow the Lord from a distance.

(Proverbs 3:5–6 KJV) 5 Trust in the LORD with all thine heart; and lean not unto thine own understanding.

6 In all thy ways acknowledge him, and he shall direct thy paths.

7 Be not wise in thine own eyes: fear the LORD, and depart from evil.

Following the Lord from a distance implies disassociation and coldness in the relationship. I call them "undercover Christians." They are Christians in name only, nothing more. Always remember this: "Our relationship with the Lord will affect our relationship with our mate."

When those individuals holding a position in our church want to take a break from ministry, some of their excuses have been: "I just want to relax. I am so busy. There are matters I must take care of." Now, I am not saying that a Christian cannot take a sabbatical to seek God and refocus, but I am advising to take caution when doing so.

THE 4-STEP PROCESS TO FOLLOWING FROM AFAR

Peter the apostle is a prime example of this process.

In (Mark 14:27–29,45–47, 54, 67–71 KJV), we read the account:

27 And Jesus saith unto them, All ye shall be offended because of me this night: for it is written, I will smite the shepherd, and the sheep shall be scattered.

28 But after that I am risen, I will go before you into Galilee. 29 But Peter said unto him, although all shall be offended, yet *will* not I. You and I claim to be followers of Jesus – not physically but relationally.

Peter became self-confident and prideful.

45 And as soon as he was come, he goeth straightway to him, and saith, Master, master; and kissed him.

46 And they laid their hands on him, and took him.

47 And one of them that stood by drew a sword, and smote a servant of the high priest, and cut off his ear.

Peter began to act out in the flesh and operate on his own behalf.

54 And Peter followed him afar off, even into the palace of the high priest: and he sat with the servants, and warmed himself at the fire.

Peter lost his fiery passion and love for the things of God and warmed himself at the enemies' fire!

67 And when she saw Peter warming himself, she looked upon him, and said, and thou also wast with Jesus of Nazareth.

68 But he denied, saying, I know not, neither understand I what thou sayest.

69 And a maid saw him again, and began to say to them that stood by, this is *one* of them.

70 And he denied it again. And a little after, they that stood by said again to Peter, Surely thou art *one* of them: for thou art a Galilaean, and thy speech agreeth *thereto*.

71 But he began to curse and to swear, *saying*, I know not this man of whom ye speak.

Peter publicly disassociated himself from Jesus.

The process is the same in the house of God.
THEY GO FROM THE PLATFORM TO THE PEW
THEY GO FROM THE PEW TO THE PARKING LOT

THEY GO FROM THE PARKING LOT TO THE PRISON (Spiritually speaking – back in bondage.)

7. Don't make choices when you're alone.

(Proverbs 11:14 AMP) Where there is no [wise, intelligent] guidance, the people fall [and go off course like a ship without a helm, But in the abundance of [wise and godly] counselors there is victory.

It is important to remember this: "No man is an island." This implies that we all need counsel and godly advice from those over us in the Lord. Take a lesson from Solomon, King David's son, who would rather take advice from his friends than from the elders of Israel, and paid dearly.

(Gen 2:18 KJV) And the LORD God said, *It is* not good that the man should be alone; I will make him an help meet for him.

This is a principle of life. God created us all to be interactive and interdependent. The Body of Christ is "many members, yet one body."

(Ecclesiastes 4:9–12 AMP) 9 Two are better than one because they have a more satisfying return for their labor; 10 for if [a]either of them falls, the one will lift up his companion. But woe to him who is alone when he falls and does not have another to lift him up. 11 Again, if two lie down together, then they keep warm; but how can one be warm *alone*? 12 And though one can overpower him who is alone, two can resist him. A cord of three *strands* is not quickly broken.

REWARD, ADVERSITY, COMFORT, STRENGTH

Remember this: "He that walks with wise men shall be wise, but a companion of fools shall be destroyed."

It is time to make wise choices for our family!

CHALLENGE

Pray together for one week and ask your Heavenly Father to give you wisdom in all your decisions.

TIME TO SUM IT ALL UP!

1. Write one word that summarizes Chapter Seven.

2. If you were a counselor, what advice would you give to a struggling couple after you read Chapter Seven?

3. Did you learn anything new?

4. What three things are we constantly reminded to do in the Book of Proverbs?

5. What is knowledge and what is wisdom?

6. Why are we encouraged in Proverbs not to make choices to quickly?

7. Why should we, as a married couple, consult God before making a decision?

8. What does it mean to "follow the crowd?"

9. What is the three-step warning in Psalms 1?

10. Why is it important to keep your guard up in your marriage relationship?

Chapter Eight

ALL WE HAVE IS TIME

MAKE THE BED, GET READY for work, make breakfast, mow the lawn, clean the garage, fix the fence, paint the interior of the house, put gas in the car, pick up the cleaning, take the kids to school, go grocery shopping, get a haircut, clean the house and take a shower. HAVE I FORGOTTEN ANYTHING?

OH YEAH! Take the kids to basketball practice, go to the dentist, get new tires for the car, pay the bills, find a baby sitter for this weekend, clean out the fireplace, plan our lesson for church, plant the new flowers in the backyard, and the list goes on and on!

So what do we do about building a meaningful relationship with our spouse and kids? WE MAKE TIME! One thing I discovered a long time ago is that somehow we manage to find the time to do the things we love to do. Regardless of the business of our daily schedules, we always make the time. What could be more important than scheduling time for the ones we love the most? Believe me, it will make all the difference in the world.

There are a variety of ways we can strengthen our relationship and build a healthy, vibrant marriage that will be lasting and satisfying.

THE REMOTE-CONTROL MARRIAGE

We are so spoiled in our new age of technology that we get irritated at the least inconvenience. Just the other day I wanted to change channels as I watched TV, but there was only one thing stopping me: I could not find the remote control! You know what I'm talking about; it's eight inches by two inches with dozens of buttons. The TV was only about eight feet in front of me; however, I didn't really want the exercise, so I yelled for my wife, "Where's the remote?"

Remember the days of no remote control for your television? You had to actually get off your backside, walk a few steps, reach out with your arm, stick out your finger, and manually change the channel? It was probably the most exercise you had in about a month! I believe our generation has become used to not having to hardly lift a finger to function daily.

I'm afraid this mindset has crept into our marriages and relationships. Here are a few reasons why some have struggling marriages.

We don't want to be inconvenienced.

We don't want to make the effort.

We want to take the shortcut.

We are just plain lazy!

THE FAVORITE REMOTE BUTTONS FOR A MAN

1. **Fast-Forward Button** – While your wife is talking to you this function moves your wife quickly to the point she is trying to make. The only problem with this is, to your wife everything she has to say is important!

   Answer: Put down the remote, focus, and pay attention. Your wife is looking for someone to listen to her.

2. **Stop Button** – This function allows life to just stop. We now can relax, vegetate, go into our shell like a turtle, and not be bothered by anyone.

   Answer: Put down the remote and let your wife into your world. Be willing to reach deep down and share a part of your heart with her.

Remember, if you give her a little bit of your heart, she will give you all of hers.

3. **Mute Button** – This button, when pushed, places you in your speechless mode. Men love to be speechless. Once they have already spoken their 12,000 words by 5:00 p.m., they arrive home in this function.

   Answer: Put down the remote and open your mouth. There are a few more grunts, snorts, and yes dears left inside of you. Give your wife the attention she needs.

4. **Power Button** – Men love this button because they always want to throw around their weight. They pride themselves in always being right, and they love to show off their physical strength.

   Answer: Put down the remote by showing your soft side. Yes, there is a part of you that is caring and kind! Remember, there is no such thing as feminine or masculine emotions, only human emotions. Your wife already knows how strong you are, but does she know how tender you are? Keep your finger off this button!

THE FAVORITE REMOTE BUTTONS FOR A WOMAN

Pause Button – This button allows women to stop and soak in the moment. By doing this they can take in every detail and experience everything there is to enjoy. Of course you know this would kill a man because most men are not detailed and they have emotions, but they would rather not use them.

Answer: When you hit the pause button, let your husband know what you are doing. Allow him to be who he is while you escape to this place of paradise. Only share bits and pieces with your spouse, because this may spark his curiosity to peer inside.

Record Button – This button allows you to file a special event or experience to watch at a later date. The record button is like a journal to a woman. My wife Marilyn is a journal addict! She began one journal a few years ago called "One Thousand Gifts." This journal is for jotting down three things you are thankful for each day. Marilyn presently has over six thousand four hundred things she is thankful for. She talked me into starting one of these journals, but I barely made it past one hundred and almost died! Do you want to know what I'm thankful for? Food, air, and Marilyn, Amen!

Rewind Button – Every woman loves this button because it allows her not only to repeat a story, but also to experience all the feelings, emotions, and passion while she is sharing it. My wife is famous for telling the same story to eight different people by eleven o'clock in the morning. Each time she tells it she adds a different sound and animation with it. I let everyone know that I'm married to a great actress!

Answer: When in this mode and you are sharing a story about your husband, please don't over-emphasize his part because you make him sound and look like a girl!

DVR Recorded Program Button – This button allows women to save a variety of different programs that she can access to match the mood she is in at that particular time. I can walk into our living room in May and Marilyn will be watching a Christmas movie! The real danger about this button is they give you the option to record any particular program whenever it comes on. Why is it dangerous, you ask? Your wife can automatically record every Hallmark movie at the push of a button!

If you have a "Woe is me" attitude concerning your marriage, then start over again. There is a "reset" button on the controller; it's called GRACE! Every morning grants us a fresh opportunity to start over again. A new day with new blessings awaiting any married couple to live and learn, forgive and be forgiven.

What I want you to notice is, for men, the remote control is negative behavior, but for women, it is positive. What does this mean for men? Let your wife have the remote!

You either build on every experience in life

Or…

You start all over again on every experience in life.

THE BUILDING BLOCKS OF LIFE – CELLS

Cells are called the building blocks of life because they are the basic unit for all living things, and must be present to make life possible.

Cells are the smallest unit of life that can reproduce independently. New cells must be created from cells that already exist. Regardless of modern science, scientists are not able to create or produce a live cell in a laboratory. There are literally trillions of cells in the human body. However, it only takes one cell to create havoc within the complex human system.

WHAT HAPPENS WHEN A CELL BECOMES STAGNANT?

A cell that is not in motion is not a productive member of the system (family). What happens then is other cells have to pick up the slack. The truth is, the other cells do not take up the slack and this is detrimental to the body. The question is, what then happens when this occurs? Rather than becoming a productive cell, they begin to imitate the useless cell and are joined to the disloyal and unproductive cell. As other cells are drafted to these useless cells, a tumor is then formed and the whole organism begins to die. It is called CANCER!

HOW TO BUILD HEALTHY CELLS IN YOUR BODY (family)

Believe it or not, each of us have anywhere between sixty to one hundred trillion cells in our body. Every twenty-four hours approximately four hundred billion cells perish and new cells take their place.

This is the secret to rejuvenating and renewing your body to remain young and healthy. If you desire a stronger or a better functioning body next year, you must concentrate and focus on regenerating your cells on a regular basis. This means eating and doing the right things.

We can now compare this to building a healthy marriage. We cannot allow ourselves to become stagnant, motionless, or disloyal in our relationships in our home, basically not contributing anything to the body but becoming detrimental and cancerous to our family!

How To Build a New Body: (Marriage)

HOW OFTEN DO CELLS REPLACE THEMSELVES?

Your outer layer of skin replaces itself every thirty-five days. We can relate this to rejuvenating our family through touch. If you read the New Testament, Jesus was touching people on a continual basis. He touched their ears, eyes, hands, head, feet, and so much more. In (Luke 4:40 KJV) it says, "Now when the sun was setting, all they that had any sick with various diseases brought them unto him; and he laid his hands on every one of them, and healed them."

Recent documented studies have revealed the benefits of emotional and physical health that are the results from human touch. Touch is one of the vital and necessary building blocks to bonding, communication, and overall health.

If both scientific and religious findings reveal the importance of human touch it would be wise to practice embracing our family at every opportunity.

Our heart cells are replaced every seven to nine months.

We can relate this to keeping our spiritual hearts tender and open in our marriage through a vibrant relationship with the Lord. When the Bible gives reference to the heart, he is not referring to our biological, beating heart, but rather is speaking about our inner spiritual life.

INNER MAN: (Ephesians 3:16 KJV) that He would grant you, according to the riches of His glory, to be strengthened with power through His Spirit in the inner man.

THE HEART OF MAN: (Psalms 119:11 KJV) Thy word have I hid in mine heart, that I might not sin against thee.

THE SPIRIT OF MAN: (I Corinthians 2:11 KJV) For what man knoweth the things of a man, save the spirit of man which is in him? even so the things of God knoweth no man, but the Spirit of God.

These scriptures imply that God communicates and relates to us through our spiritual lives (heart). If it is the life of God that gives life to the marriage union, we must continually revitalize our relationship with our spouse through allowing God's Spirit to refresh and renew it. Actually, biological health is at its peak when every member of the human body lives unselfishly for every other member of the body.

The problem with two individuals joined together by God through a holy covenant is, even though God makes two of them one, they are still two distinctive individuals. Even though they are one in marriage, they have their own likes and dislikes and their different ways of thinking and doing. This can be a recipe for chaos and confusion if we are set on always getting our way. The most effective way to solve this issue is to open our hearts and put each other first. Why? Because marriage is a great place to practice unselfishness, which will produce a healthy marriage!

Our entire skeletal structures are regenerated every three months.

We can relate this through allowing the word of God to bring stability and strength to our marriage relationship. The scripture says in (Hebrews

4:12 KJV) "For the word of God *is* living and powerful, and sharper than any two-edged sword, piercing even to the division of soul and spirit, and of joints and marrow, and is a discerner of the thoughts and intents of the heart."

(Ephesians 2:20–21 AMP) 20 having been built on the foundation of the apostles and prophets, with Christ Jesus Himself as the [Chief] Cornerstone, 21 in whom the whole structure is joined together, and it continues [to increase] growing into a holy temple in the Lord [a sanctuary dedicated, set apart, and sacred to the presence of the Lord].

The King James Version uses the words "fitly framed together," suggesting the framework that is joined is interlocked and fastened to one another.

When one member suffers, we all suffer. This most certainly applies to the marriage union, "The Timepiece of God."

CHALLENGE:

Plan a regular date night. Discuss various ways each of you can build loyalty and trust in the marriage.

TIME TO SUM IT ALL UP!

1. Write one word that summarizes Chapter Eight.

2. If you were a counselor, what advice would you give to a struggling couple after you read Chapter Eight?

3. Did you learn anything new?

4. What are the favorite buttons on the remote control for the man and why?

5. What are the favorite buttons on a remote control for the woman and why?

6. What are the building blocks of life?

7. What happens when a cell becomes stagnant and disloyal and how can this be applied to the marriage relationship?

8. How can we build healthy cells in our bodies and how does this apply to marriage?

9. What are the three aspects in scripture concerning our spiritual life?

10. How can we bring stability and strength to our marriage relationship?

Chapter Nine

A TIME OF HAPPINESS

What is the first thing that comes to your mind when I say the word "happiness?" Is it the end of the workweek, because people are unhappy at work but they love the weekends? Is it a special vacation in the Bahamas, Hawaii, or possibly a cruise to the Caribbean? Is it a midday nap, or possibly happy hour at the local bar? Is it being married or single, a parent or kid-less?

Whatever the case, I want to present the Bible's perspective concerning "true happiness."

There are two words translated as "happiness." The first word is translated "happiness," the emotion of happiness, which is defined as a brief state of emotional elation. In Hebrew, this happiness is translated (seem-KHAH).

And then there's joy of the long term, a less emotional but more constant state of contentment and peace. It is translated OH-shehr, and is pronounced in some instances as the word "gain or wealth."

Depending on the translation, the Bible uses the words "happy" and "happiness" in various instances around thirty times, but uses the words "joy" and "rejoice" over three hundred times.

This reveals a truth that we must all understand, because the majority of the people in the United States, the most prosperous nation on planet Earth, are so unhappy. I remember seeing a couple at a restaurant talking, and one said to their mate, "You don't make me happy." I almost went over to them and said, if you're basing your happiness on the behavior of others you are going to be unhappy 99% of the time. This is where so many married couples get off track, because they are waiting for their mate to make them happy. If you tied the knot in marriage to find happiness, I know you have not found it yet! Happiness cannot be found in people because there are no perfect people on planet Earth.

We must first establish what happiness is not.

Happiness is not a…

PLACE

Happiness is not in a geographical location, because if it were you would have to spend your life at the happiest place, on earth, Disneyland! I have known couples and individuals that are only happy when they are on vacation. Europe, Jerusalem, Alaska, the tropics, to name a few, along with thousands of dollars spent, only to find that happiness could not come home with them!

EVENT

An event is defined as…

- something that happens
- an occurrence
- a happening
- a social activity

Or, if you're an educated nut, this one's for you!

- the fundamental entity of observed physical reality represented by a point designated by three coordinates of place and one of time

Wow, my head hurts just thinking about it! You cannot find happiness at a picnic, swap meet, sports venue, wedding, or even the biggest roller coaster on the planet!

CIRCUMSTANCE

The Happiness Of Circumstance

I've noticed certain people that are only happy if their circumstances are perfect. I hope you know where I am going with this because most of the time these people are very unhappy.

If you are waiting for your circumstances to change in order to be a happy person, you are going to be waiting a long time. If you're waiting for everything to go your way and to get your ducks in a row, I have a news flash for you: ducks are out of season!

The truth is, happiness cannot be found in a place, event, or in your circumstances being perfect. Why? Because happiness is not external. Just ask Hollywood. They have the world at their fingertips, all they could ask for, and everything their heart desires, and they are still extremely miserable.

Just ask King Solomon about happiness because he will tell you the truth. Let's read.

(Ecclesiastes 2:7–11 KJV)

7 I got *me* servants and maidens, and had servants born in my house; also I had great possessions of great and small cattle above all that were in Jerusalem before me:

8 I gathered me also silver and gold, and the peculiar treasure of kings and of the provinces: I got me men singers and women singers, and the delights of the sons of men, *as* musical instruments, and that of all sorts.

9 So I was great, and increased more than all that were before me in Jerusalem: also my wisdom remained with me.

10 And whatsoever mine eyes desired I kept not from them, I withheld not my heart from any joy; for my heart rejoiced in all my labour: and this was my portion of all my labour.

11 Then I looked on all the works that my hands had wrought, and on the labour that I had laboured to do: and, behold, all *was* vanity and vexation of spirit, and *there was* no profit under the sun.

As King Solomon looked across the horizon, he had obtained everything a man could possibly desire. Wouldn't that be wonderful? Not according to Solomon! What was his conclusion to finding happiness and fulfillment in life? Everything he had acquired was empty and useless. He had it, but he did not enjoy it! Why? His heart had been severed from his real purpose in life. What was that purpose? I believe it was to share God's glory through heaven.

(1 Kings 11:3–5 AMP) 3 He had seven hundred wives, princesses, and three hundred concubines, and his wives turned his heart away [from God]. 4 For when Solomon was old, his wives turned his heart away after other gods; and his heart was not completely devoted to the LORD HIS GOD, AS WAS THE HEART OF HIS FATHER DAVID. 5 For Solomon went after Ashtoreth, the [fertility] goddess of the Sidonians, and after Milcom the horror (detestable idol) of the Ammonites

Both of these lifeless gods included sexual worship. Indeed, Solomon had lost his purpose because Jehovah's "blessing" would be through his descendants and lineage, of which these idol gods required child sacrifice and immoral acts.

They had turned his heart and head away from his relationship with God through pride and luxury. The things that God had provided him to "enjoy" now became his burden. The scripture says in 1 Timothy 6:17 (KJV),

"Charge them that are rich in this world, that they be not high minded, nor trust in uncertain riches, but in the living God, who giveth us richly all things to enjoy."

Basically, Solomon became arrogant and worldly and therefore could not enjoy the things that God had given him to enjoy.

As a married couple we must not lose our focus and place our hearts upon the provision of the Lord. There's a timeless quote that says, "We should not love things and use people, but we should love people and use things." There's nothing wrong with having "stuff," just don't let the stuff have you!

WHAT IS HAPPINESS?

HAPPINESS IS A STATE OF MIND

Close your eyes and imagine you are on your favorite beach anywhere in the entire world. While you sip your iced tea, a fresh breeze blows through your hair. You listen to the pleasant waves roll slowly upon the sandy beach as the sun peeks through the palm trees. Far in the distance you recognize your favorite love song being played as you begin to doze off.

How do you feel now? Notice how your heartbeat lowered, your tension lessened, and your body began to relax. Why? I always say, "Wherever your mind goes, your body will follow." This is a Bible truth that the apostle Paul only knew too well. In Philippians 4:8 (AMP) it says, "Finally, believers, whatever is true, whatever is honorable and worthy of respect, whatever is right and confirmed by God's word, whatever is pure and wholesome, whatever is lovely and brings peace, whatever is admirable and of good repute; if there is any excellence, if there is anything worthy of praise, think continually on these things [center your mind on them, and implant them in your heart]."

This is why he could sit in a Roman prison, bruised and beaten, and sing the "Song of the Lord." This is why he could declare with confidence, "For me to live is Christ, and to die is gain." Paul brings us to the conclusion that happiness "is a choice."

The Bible discipline of right thinking produces great blessings. Isaiah 26:3 (ESV) says, "You will keep him in perfect peace whose mind is stayed on you."

The couple whose focus and mind is continually occupied with the things of God will have perfect peace instead of anxiety. Paul says thinking on right things and practicing them brings the God of peace. So many are missing the joy of living and are unhappy because their thoughts are deceiving them concerning true happiness.

WHEN YOU LOSE

We live in a win-win world. In our upbringing we are taught to win at any cost. To be the best you have to beat the best. Normally people associate losing with losers. People who are not champions and winners in life. This could not be further from the truth, because Christ declared, "If you want to live, you die, and if you want to gain you lose."

WHAT DOES THIS MEAN?

There is more value when you lose.

There is multiplication when you lose.

There is greater experience when you lose.

When you read the stories and experiences of our forefathers, the greatest lessons learned and perspective gained were during times of loss and adversity. The majority of the great hymns of God were written out of loss and hardship.

THE ATTITUDE OF LOSING

The truth is we lose many more times in life than we win. Math is a universal truth, and it is rarely ever wrong. Each time a gambler makes a bet at a casino, the odds are against him, every time! The casino is not in the habit of losing and is confident that over time they won't lose against the gamblers. The odds at winning at slot machines are one in 5,000, with a chance of one in about 34 million at winning the big prize.

Just ask honest Abe Lincoln, who lost jobs, failed in business, lost his girl by death, had a nervous breakdown, was defeated for senate, congress, speaker, and was defeated for nomination as Vice President before becoming our president.

This should help our perspective in life and help our attitudes and overall outlook to be positive and upbeat.

HAPPINESS IS A CONDITION OF HEART

We are commanded in the scriptures to "Rejoice in the Lord, always, and receive the joy of the Lord as our strength." These scriptures reveal that our "happiness" and "joy" are found in our positional relationship with our creator. In the beginning Adam and Eve "walked with God" in the garden." The "joy" of the garden was experienced as God walked with them in the garden he had provided. We are also commanded in scripture to be content, thankful, and joyful where we are at right now. That is exactly why happiness cannot be found in a place, event, or circumstance. These elements are constantly changing like the weather and cannot be relied upon or trusted.

Therefore, we can rejoice and be glad in whatever circumstance and place we are in at this present time, because our happiness is in a God who changes not!

Notice the conversation between Gabriel and Mary in

(Luke 1: 28-35 KJV)

28 And the angel came in unto her, and said, Hail, *thou that art* highly favoured, the Lord *is* with thee: blessed *art* thou among women.

29 And when she saw *him*, she was troubled at his saying, and cast in her mind what manner of salutation this should be.

30 And the angel said unto her, Fear not, Mary: for thou hast found favour with God.

31 And, behold, thou shalt conceive in thy womb, and bring forth a son, and shalt call his name JESUS.

32 He shall be great, and shall be called the Son of the Highest: and the Lord God shall give unto him the throne of his father David:

33 And he shall reign over the house of Jacob forever; and of his kingdom there shall be no end.

34 Then said Mary unto the angel, How shall this be, seeing I know not a man?

35 And the angel answered and said unto her, The Holy Ghost shall come upon thee, and the power of the Highest shall overshadow thee: therefore also that holy thing which shall be born of thee shall be called the Son of God.

IN WHAT MANNER DID THE ANGEL SPEAK TO MARY?

(Verse 28) He validated her importance.

(Verse 30) He vanquished her fear.

(Verse 31) He imparted a gift to her.

(Verses 32–33) He spoke into her future.

(Verses 34–35) He spoke detailed and comforting words to her.

Now notice the drastic contrast between the conversation between Gabriel and Joseph in (Matthew 1:18–21 KJV):

18 Now the birth of Jesus Christ was on this wise: When as his mother Mary was espoused to Joseph, before they came together, she was found with child of the Holy Ghost.

19 Then Joseph her husband, being a just *man*, and not willing to make her a public example, was minded to put her away privily.

20 But while he thought on these things, behold, the angel of the Lord appeared unto him in a dream, saying, Joseph, thou son of David, fear not to take unto thee Mary thy wife: for that which is conceived in her is of the Holy Ghost.

21 And she shall bring forth a son, and thou shalt call his name JESUS: for he shall save his people from their sins.

Notice there were no specifics, only commands:

(Verse 20) I want you to marry Mary.
(Verse 21) I want you to name the baby Jesus.

When the Lord spoke once again to Joseph in (Matthew 2:13 (a)(b) KJV), he said, "13 Arise, and take the young child and his mother, and flee into Egypt, and be thou there until I bring thee word: for Herod will seek the young child to destroy him."

There were no specifics, just commands. With Mary there was details, details, details! Men, when it comes to women, take your time, be animated, and don't leave any details out. Women, when it comes to men, just get to the point. That's the way it is and that's the way we like it!

I hope this book has been a blessing to you and your marriage. "Always remember: In marriage, You always have a dance partner, You can always drive in the commute lane, You always have a dinner date, and You always have a warm bed." Always remember, the Marriage Maker Himself is God and He would like to declare over you, "And They Lived Happily Ever After."

TIME TO SUM IT ALL UP!

1. Write one word that summarizes Chapter Nine.

2. If you were a counselor, what advice would you give to a struggling couple after you read Chapter Nine?

3. Did you learn anything new?

4. Finish this statement:
Happiness is not a…

5. What is happiness?

6. True or false?

Happiness is external. True ( ) False ( )

Happiness is a choice. True ( ) False ( )

7. What is the difference between winning and losing?

8. What should our attitude be when we lose?

9. Like Gabriel the archangel spoke to Mary, in what manner are we supposed to speak to our wives?

10. How did the angel Gabriel address Joseph?

RATING THIS BOOK: Thank you for purchasing this book for the sole purpose of strengthening, enhancing, and building your relationship with your lifelong marriage partner. My prayer and heart's delight is that your marriage will become all that God intended it to be and do.

In order to survey the impact of this book, please take ten minutes of your time to grade the effectiveness of each chapter. By answering ten questions about the contents of this book, this will help in writing future books and will help millions of others to join our mission in saving the marriages in America and around the world.

(1) Was the book practical and easy to read? Yes No

(2) Note one thing you learned that was new and exciting that you could apply to your marriage today?

(3) Did the book draw you into the storyline, where you became a part of the message? Yes No

(4) Did the book encourage you to do better in your marriage? Yes No

(5) Was the book Biblical? Yes No

(6) Would you read this book again to tune up your marriage? Yes No

(7) Was the book user-friendly? Yes No

(8) Would you recommend this book to your friends? Yes No

(9) Is this book helping you to build your marriage God's way? Yes No

(10) Could you use this book to start your own marriage study in your home or in your church? Yes No

Thank you for becoming an advocate in restoring God's original plan for marriage. Through your feedback and response, we can send a message to our culture that marriage is the most important relationship in God's creation, and together change the landscape of our society to reflect Christ and His church. Please visit our Facebook page: The Marriage Maker – "What Time Is It In Your Marriage?"

All comments and questions are welcome!

For information, books, or booking a marriage conference, please call or write…

Family Celebration Center

5045 Fulton Drive, Suite E

Fairfield, CA 94534 (Located in Cordelia Junction)

Direct: 707-864-5653

Email: fccojeda@aol.com

BOOKS:

What In The World Was God Thinking? "Marriage"

The Marriage Maker

FUTURE PROJECTS:

"Laugh Attack"
   (8 Ways To Better Your Marriage Through Laughter)

"Marriage, God's Masterpiece of Himself"
   (A Refection in the Mind of God)

"Warrior/Princess"
   (Two Lives, Two Hearts, One Mission)

"Marilyn & Me"
   (A 40-Year Journey Through Marriage)

"Bite-Size Devotional"
   (For Those Who Like To Eat On The Run)

ABOUT THE AUTHOR

GREG OJEDA is the Senior Pastor at Family Celebration Center and the author of the book What in the World Was God Thinking? "Marriage." Greg has ministered in the cities of Fairfield, Suisun, and Cordelia for over thirty-seven years. He specializes in family and marriage counseling as well as leadership and pastoral development. His interests are speed-reading, painting, music, and weight-lifting.

Greg always says, "Marriage is not for the faint of heart," because it takes Courage, Commitment, and Character to guard this precious treasure from God. This "Warrior and Princess" union calls for toughness and tenderness, strength and submission, honor and humility to conquer the world given to its responsibility.

"In marriage: You always have a dance partner, You can always drive in the carpool lane, You always have a dinner date, and You always have a warm bed." Always remember, the Marriage Maker Himself is God, and He would like to declare over you, "And They Lived Happily Ever After."